U.S. Trade in the Sixties and Seventies

U.S. Trade in the Sixties and Seventies

Continuity and Change

Edited by
Kenneth Jameson
Roger Skurski
University of Notre Dame

Lexington Books
D.C. Heath and Company
Lexington, Massachusetts
Toronto   London

Library of Congress Cataloging in Publication Data

Main entry under title:

U.S. trade in the sixties and seventies.

Based on a conference on emerging international trade patterns of the
U.S., University of Notre Dame, Apr. 1973.
1. United States—Commerce—Congresses. I. Jameson, Kenneth,
1942- ed. II. Skurski, Roger, ed.
HF3008.U5   382'.0973   73-22012
ISBN 0-669-92692-2

Published simultaneously in Canada.

Printed in the United States of America.

International Standard Book Number: 0-669-92692-2

Library of Congress Catalog Card Number: 73-22012

To Penny, Maureen, Rex, Michael,
Kevin, Matthew, and Tanya

Contents

List of Figures

List of Tables

Preface

International economic affairs have occupied an unaccustomed, prominent place in the recent economic concerns of the United States. Testimony to this is the frequent reference to the "crisis" in international payments or international monetary relations.

While we have all become accustomed to "crises" to the extent of considering them rhetorical devices, whatever sense of crisis we do feel stems from our general inattention to the underlying trends in international economic relations and our surprise when they impinge upon us. There is no need for this; the causes of the present crisis have long been evolving, and the surprising aspect is that we have not spent more time in investigating and understanding them. This book attempts to fill this gap by bringing together studies on the underlying trading relations between the United States and her major world trading partners.

The book is based on a conference on "Emerging International Trade Patterns of the United States" which was held at the University of Notre Dame in April 1973. The conference was first proposed by Dr. Stephen Kertesz, Chairman of the Institute for International Studies of the University of Notre Dame, whose broad experience in international affairs has constantly reminded him of the central role of trade in international relations. The Institute sponsored the conference, and it was organized by the Department of Economics under its chairman, Dr. Dennis Dugan.

The chapters in this volume are revised versions of papers presented at the conference, revised to take into account the comments of the other participants as well as recent developments in international trading relations. We would like to thank the Association of Comparative Economic Studies for permission to use copyrighted material from the Spring 1973 issue of *The ACES Bulletin.*

1

Introduction

American consumers want to buy imported products from time to time. . . .
But American consumers want to know where the imported unit and its parts
were made and not be fooled by an American brand name on the front.

—United States Senator Vance Hartke (Ind.)
September 28, 1971

During most of the period since the end of the Second World War, the United
States has been in an enviable position in terms of her international trading
relations. Every year through 1970 she had run a surplus in terms of goods and
services reaching as high as $11.6 billion dollars in one year. With the help of the
exchange earned in this manner, the United States has been able to undertake
large amounts of foreign investment and a wide range of additional foreign
involvements.

The kind treatment which the trading sphere accorded the United States
seems to be gone forever. The prospect of our first deficit in trade of goods and
services can plausibly be cited as a precipitating factor in the first round of
"Nixon economic medicine" applied to the economy in August 1971. For it was
that realization which forced the United States into taking more dramatic steps
to begin to control her domestic economy and thereby to regain control over her
international trading relations. Such control has to date not been reestablished,
although the balance on goods and services is beginning to show a surplus again.

The effects of these developments are by now well known. The disarray in
international monetary arrangements has been the subject of several efforts at
order: the Smithsonian Agreement in December 1971, which in effect was a
devaluation of the dollar; the agreement among the European countries of the
Common Market to maintain parity among their currencies; the subsequent
dollar devaluation of March 1973, with the European joint float and the
Japanese and British float of their currencies. Of course all this took place
against the backdrop of the first effort to develop a new international monetary
system in Nairobi in the fall of 1973 and the first hesitant steps toward more
trade liberalization.

This book takes these efforts as data in its concern with the "real" side of
international relations, the trade in goods and services. For while the overall
stability and balance in the international economy is greatly conditioned by the

1

type of monetary arrangements in effect, the pressure on those arrangements and the effects which trade can have on a domestic economy are greatly influenced by the real side of trade. It is also in this area that many interesting changes occurred during the 1960s, changes which will condition international economic relations during the 1970s no matter what form of monetary agreement is reached.

Referring back to the statement of the Senator from Indiana, we can see that he understates the case, that during the 1960s in particular the United States citizen became more than a little accustomed to buying imported goods, particularly manufactured goods. For in international trade this was the area of most rapid growth, and the United States was no exception. Thus, familiarity with Japanese television sets and German cars, not to mention Italian shoes and French wine, has probably conditioned the extent to which small monetary adjustments can bring about balance in trade; it has changed the "elasticities" of these products. Or take the second part of the statement. One might want to know where a product had been made, but during the 1960s we saw the growth of the multinational firm which might purchase component parts in Germany, the United States, Brazil, and France—and then assemble them in Taiwan or the Dominican Republic for export to the United States. It would of course be impossible to mark this product with its "country of origin." A similar influence has been in the expansion of the numbers and types of trading partners as we have moved to normalization of trade with virtually every country in the world except Cuba. Such a multitude of trading partners would again make it difficult for the customers to keep track of the origins of their goods. But these are only two of the many changes in trading relations which occurred during the 1960s and which will continue to influence trade in the 1970s.

Furthermore, there is an entirely different reason for taking trade as a topic of interest in itself, and this is its basic role in international relations. One key aspect is that trade does facilitate a basic increase in the welfare of the world economy by promoting a more efficient use of resources. The gains to the efficiency of operation of the world economy should by now be obvious. But there are other dimensions in the economic sphere affected by trade relations.

In a smaller, less developed economy, the patterns of trade may be the dominant factor in setting the growth path for the economy. For example, both the terms of trade consideration and the difference in linkages between primary and manufactured exports provide a strong presumption that the growth of a modern economy will be hampered by sole reliance on primary exports.

Analysis of trade is also fundamental for reasons growing out of the basic structure of international relations. History has demonstrated that trade agreements and trade relations can be major influences on the entire fabric of international relations. The case of the Soviet Union and the thaw in its relations with the United States has at least been facilitated by the trade agreements reached, and it can be claimed that the desirability of trade provided a motive force for the thaw in the first place. While such dramatic developments as those with the Soviet Union and China are unlikely to recur with great frequency, they do serve to highlight that trade, by its nature, can be a major factor contributing to the maintenance of stable international relations. There are deviations from this, as in the Central American conflict between Honduras and El Salvador, but in general the pressure of trade for peaceful relations is a major one, which makes it all the more important to understand the trends in trade and the major factors determining those trends.

Turning from the overall importance of trade to the postwar trends which must be accounted for in understanding United States trading relationships, perhaps the major development has been the very rapid rise in international trade, a rise far outdistancing the rise in world output. The implication of course is that the economies of the world are becoming less self-sufficient and more dependent on each other for their goods, and this would also suggest that the earth's resources are being used in a more efficient manner. This is made most clear by the increased participation of the Soviet Union and the United States in international trade. They are the two largest economies on the globe and the two with the greatest potential for self-sufficiency, yet the share of trade in their total GNP is increasing. Some attempts may be made to slow this growth, such as the Nixon energy policy which seems to aim for self-sufficiency, but the overall development is unlikely to be reversed.

A second main theme which emerges from a careful consideration of developments during the 1960s is the increase in the various dimensions in which countries are interrelated. The rise of the multinational firm, the spread of joint development projects, the international movement of labor as well as the continuation and diversification of capital movements, and the evolution of the product cycle of production and consumption are all indicators of the many forms of interdependence. In every chapter in this volume there is discussion of one or more of these dimensions and their growth during the 1960s. Each author identifies important aspects of the overall trends and attempts to specify the major factors at work in that area. As a whole the book provides a comprehensive understanding of these new developments and should allow the reader to keep pace with them and to realize the underlying patterns to the new crises which will arise in this area.

Emerging from the chapters presented here is a warning of the importance for the United States to adjust to these new developments in the international sphere because of their implications for our domestic policy. The chapters demonstrate the significance for the United States as well as other nations of an awareness and consideration of developments elsewhere, and of a closer and more effective collaboration on domestic economic policies. This collaboration as well as a new monetary system and the reduction of barriers to trade should properly be the subject of international economic discussions among the nations of the world.

The United States is now more dependent on the international sphere for its products, and this is not a trend to be feared. At the same time that international economics is causing a reorientation of our traditional friendships, we may find more agreement and cooperation in our economic relations with the Soviet Union and China than with our traditional European or Third World partners. In addition, the role of our multinational firms in these countries has been a matter of increasing criticism which may again affect us internally. Until the devaluation of the dollar, the establishment of foreign subsidiaries frequently was the only means for American firms to enter foreign markets. Now, however, the United States will be in a better position in many fields to compete in the export sector with other trading nations, and this may reduce some of the criticism of multinationals.

Additional, more comprehensive monetary adjustments may result from efforts initiated at the Nairobi meetings of the international monetary authorities, but it is unlikely that a new system will be agreed upon very soon. The implication is that the course set for us by the last decade and discussed in this book will continue to influence international developments for a considerable period of time.

2

An Overview: U.S. Foreign Trade in the 1960s and Early 1970s

James J. Rakowski
University of Notre Dame

Introduction

In taking an overview of the situation of the United States in the world economy in the past decade, we see a massive, affluent, remarkably self-sufficient economy becoming slightly more dependent upon a shrinking world and undergoing a significant shift in the composition, direction, and very nature of its international commerce.

In this chapter I will first assess the changing dependence of the United States on the world economy. Then I will attempt to delineate the changing composition of its merchandise trade. Thirdly, I will sketch the shifting directions in which its merchandise trade flows. And finally, I will suggest that the past decade has provided ample evidence that the United States' role in international commerce is much broader than can be observed down at dockside.

The Relative Dependence of the United States on the World Economy

Most American international trade textbooks begin by saying that although international trade represents a small fraction of the American GNP relative to the ratio observed in European countries or Japan, this does not imply that international trade is unimportant. I am, of course, going to give the same warning. In the first place, I am going to suggest that the United States is becoming slightly, but not dramatically, more dependent on international trade. I would like also to caution against two deceptive interpretations of figures purporting to indicate the dependence of the United States on world trade. A warning with respect to the first misinterpretation is commonly given in the trade textbooks referred to above. The second is so surprisingly seldom referred to that I might claim some small originality in its presentation.

In 1960 imports were 4.5 percent of our GNP. In 1972 imports were 5.0 percent of the GNP.[1] (In 1960 exports were slightly higher than imports, in 1972 slightly lower.) So, by this measure, the United States became slightly, but not at all dramatically, more dependent on international trade. In the world as a whole, output was growing at about the same rate as trade, so the United States' relative self-sufficiency was becoming slightly less pronounced.[2]

These figures do not mean, of course, that if the United States were suddenly isolated, its GNP would only fall by some 5 percent. This is the first warning. Deeper consideration reveals that many of our imports are intermediate products critical for the many subsequent stages of production which add value to our GNP. For example, 38 percent of the oil the United States consumes is imported; 32 percent of our iron ore is imported; 80 percent of our fluorspar; almost all of our platinum.[3] None of these commodities, of course, is completely without substitutes; but an adequately measured GNP would certainly fall far more than 5 percent were foreign trade eliminated. Other of our imports are consumer goods with no close, domestically produced substitutes. Thus, were we deprived of our daily quota of coffee, a monetary measure of our diminished sense of well-being might far exceed the 40 or 50 cents we pay for coffee.

Secondly, I wish to warn against what seems to be a common fallacy in assessing the effect of foreign influences upon the domestic goal of price stability. In particular, we should not underestimate the effect of price rises of foreign goods upon the domestic price level. A 10 percent devaluation of the dollar would, with perfectly elastic foreign supplies, increase the dollar price of our imports by 10 percent. Imports are 5 percent of our GNP. One might be tempted to estimate that the effect of a 10 percent devaluation on our domestic price level would therefore be an increase of .10 x .05 or about 0.5 percent. It would be a bit less if foreign prices tend to fall as our demand lags; it would be a bit more if imported goods are intermediate goods upon which price increases are pyramided in subsequent stages.

Such an analysis does not rest upon sound economic theory, and there is some evidence, for example, as suggested by Paul McCracken in an essay in the *Wall Street Journal*,[4] that the impact of recent devaluations upon the consumer price index has been substantial, and more than was anticipated. The crucial fact to emphasize is that for a great many products, imports represent the marginal units and bear an economic significance far beyond their percentage of total sales.[5]

Consider the domestic demand and supply schedules for a "typical import" in Figure 2-1a. By horizontally subtracting the quantity supplied from the quantity demanded we can derive an excess demand curve (*ED*) in Figure 2-1b. This excess demand is provided for by foreign supply, indicated by the arbitrarily drawn *FS* curve in Figure 2-1b. The equilibrium price *p* is thus determined. In this equilibrium, imports represent only 5 percent of total domestic sales. If the foreign supply curve is shifted up by 10 percent because of a devaluation, the equilibrium price will rise to *p'*. The extent of the price rise will be determined by the slopes of the excess demand and supply curves. If the slopes were −1 and

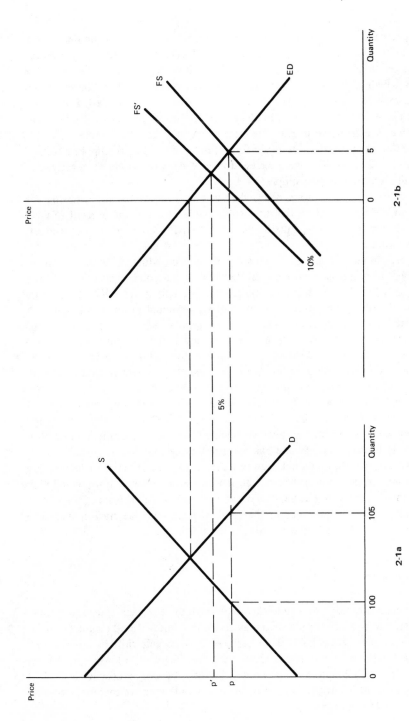

Figure 2-1. Effect of a 10 Percent Devaluation on a Relatively Self-sufficient Country

+1, respectively, the price rise would be 5 percent. The extent of the price rise is not directly affected by the percentage of total sales accounted for by imports. We can see this by looking at Figure 2-2, where we consider the case of a country which is much more dependent on international trade in the sense that imports represent a much larger percentage of quantity demanded. But in this case, if the slopes of the excess demand and foreign supply curves are the same as they were in the previous case, the price rise would again be 5 percent.

A similar analysis could be made for export goods, using the upper left-hand quadrant of the b graph, where excess domestic demand would be negative and thus really represent excess supply.

It can be seen, therefore, that what is really important for assessing the impact of a devaluation on the domestic price level is not the percent of GNP accounted for by imports, but the percent of GNP accounted for by products that are tradable.

Because some of our GNP consists of services which generally must be performed domestically, and some of the value of our goods is accounted for by service activities such as domestic transport and retailing, for which there is no effective import competition, only part of our national product is tradable. A rough and ready calculation indicates that approximately 50 percent of the goods and services which make up our GNP are tradable. And thus, assuming again just for convenience slopes of −1 and +1, the rise in our price level as the result of a 10 percent devaluation would be one-half of 5 percent or 2.5 percent, which is five times more than the estimate criticized earlier.

Although I myself will not venture a forecast as to the future, I am aware that some individuals see the United States as rapidly becoming a "have-not" nation and view with alarm the country's projected dependence upon imports. For example, in a recent speech one businessman[6] projected that our need for fuels and raw materials alone would require that our imports double, or increase by 100 percent, by the year 1985; and he saw this as a crisis which we would have to face in the next thirteen years. To put this impending crisis into perspective, it should be pointed out that in the past thirteen years we have managed to increase our imports by 260 percent![7]

Composition of U.S. Trade

Our merchandise trade is often classified into three broad categories: food, beverages, and tobacco; crude materials and fuel; manufactured products. As far as our imports are concerned, there has been a noticeable shift in composition. But it is not the shift one might expect after reading a recent Associated Press dispatch from Washington: "The United States is becoming heavily dependent on foreign countries not only for oil, but for a wide range of materials, warns a new report to the government."[8]

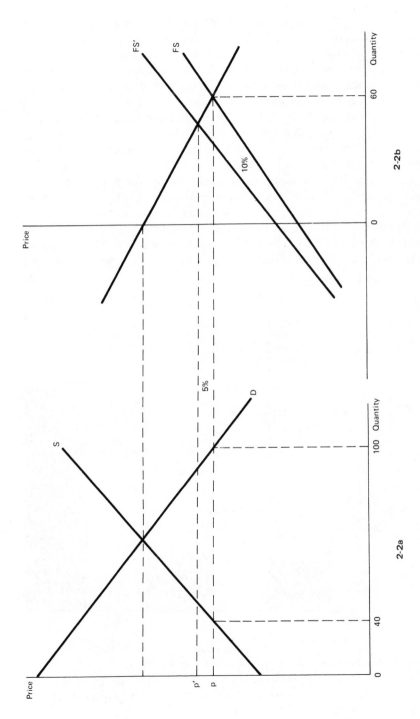

Figure 2-2. Effect of a 10 Percent Devaluation on a Relatively Trade-Dependent Country

In the past decade it has been in the third category, manufactured products, that trade has grown strikingly. The fact that manufactured products now represent a much larger percentage of our total imports is shown graphically in Figure 2-3. In absolute terms, which can be seen in Table 2-1, our imports of goods and raw materials expanded; but so did our exports and at about the same rate. In 1960 imports of food exceeded exports by a small amount. In 1972 they still did. In 1960 imports of fuel and crude materials exceeded exports by a small amount. In 1972, they still did. But in 1960 exports of manufactured goods exceeded imports by almost 100 percent. In 1972 imports exceeded exports by almost 11 percent.

I do not know if the trend will continue, but in the past decade it was certainly in the category of "manufactured products" that the most significant changes occurred. It might be worthwhile to look into this aggregate category in more detail. Two of our major manufactured product exports in 1960 held up quite well through 1972. Machinery exports increased from 4,293.6 (million dollars) to 11,560, chemicals from 1,680 to 3,836. Our increase in imports was

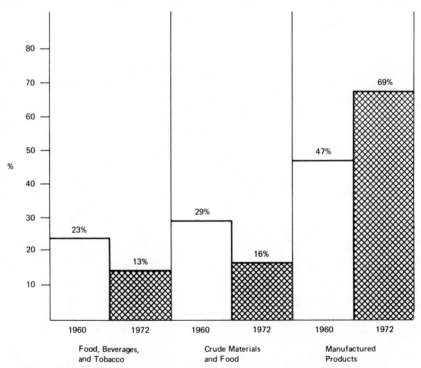

Figure 2-3. Percentage of U.S. Imports by Major Commodity Classification: 1960 and 1972. Source: Computed from U.S. Department of Commerce, *Survey of Current Business* Vol. 41, November 1961, pp. S21-2; Vol. 53, April, 1973, p. S23.

Table 2-1
Imports and Exports by Broad Classification, 1960 and 1972
(millions of dollars)

	Imports		Exports	
	1960	1972	1960	1972
Food, Beverages and Tobacco	3,392	7,371	3,107	6,573
Crude Materials and Fuels	4,418	8,839	3,942	7,090
Manufactures	6,863	37,748	12,583	33,650
Total	15,073	55,555	19,659	48,116

Source: U.S. Department of Commerce, *Survey of Current Business*, Vol. 41, November 1961, pp. S21-2; Vol. 53, April, 1973, p. S23.

scattered over a wide range of commodities, with the one notable increase of major magnitude in automobiles, which increased from a small amount not meriting separate classification to almost 7 billion dollars worth. Professor Baldwin's contribution gives us a framework in which we can analyze these shearing currents of trade in manufacturers.

The Direction of Trade

Since 1960 there has been a noticeable shift in the directions to and from which United States' trade has flowed, as shown in Figure 2-4. Looking particularly at some countries of current interest, and breaking down the aggregates shown in the table, we find that Japan has grown in importance as a trading partner. Its share of our exports grew from less than 7 percent to slightly more than 9 percent in 1971. Its share of our imports grew from about 7 percent to about 15 percent. The Soviet Union was not yet a significant factor in our trade by 1972, and the entire Soviet bloc accounted for only about $0.9 billion of our exports, or about 2 percent. In the next decade, however, we might well see an expansion of our trade with the Soviet Union more dramatic than the expansion of trade with Japan in the past decade. In Chapter 8, Professor Dernberger assesses the prospects for trade with the People's Republic of China, which through 1972 had conducted virtually no trade with the United States.

Capital Flows as a Substitute for Trade

The most dramatic change in the United States' current account since 1960 has been a tripling of the net earnings on foreign investment. We might say that one

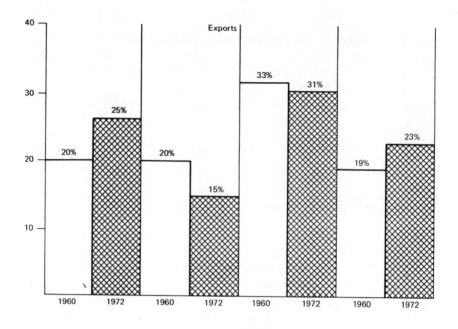

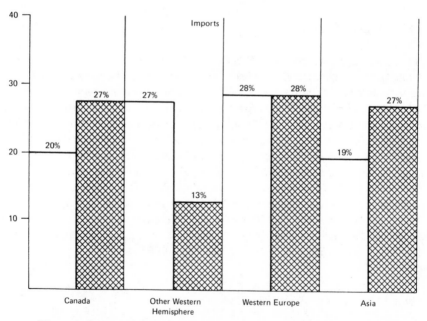

Figure 2-4. U.S. Exports and Imports: Percentage Shares by Major Trading Regions. Source: U.S. Department of Commerce, *Survey of Current Business* Vol. 41, November 1961, pp. S21-2; Vol. 53, April, 1973, p. S22.

of the United States' primary exports is now the services of capital and technology and skilled managers. In 1960 net earnings on private foreign investment were 2,825 (millions of dollars). In 1972 they were 9,211. Earnings on capital have long ago surpassed net capital outflows, which were only 632 in 1972.

There is a great debate, of course, as to what extent the export of capital and managerial services is a substitute for merchandise exports, rather than a complement. Much of the debate centers on the feasibility of exports given current artificial impediments to trade. In one sense, however, there is no doubt that the export of such services is a substitute for merchandise exports. Certainly it represents an alternative source of foreign exchange; and thus for any level of merchandise imports in excess of merchandise exports there is less need for the exchange rate to depreciate than there would be in the absence of capital earnings, and thus less of an incentive is given to exports. Put another way, without earnings from foreign investments, the recent depreciations of the dollar would have likely come sooner and been deeper, and exports would have been given even more of a stimulus than they have been given.

The growing net return to capital and managerial services recently exported from the United States is a normal phenomenon for the world in its current stage of development. It would certainly be a serious mistake to expect that all of United States merchandise import needs of the future must be covered by merchandise exports.

Summary

The following points may be made by way of summary. The United States has long been dependent upon the world economy, more so than a casual reading of the statistics might indicate. It has become slightly more dependent in the past decade, but not dramatically so. There have been marked changes in United States trade in the broad category denoted as manufactured products. A noticeable share of our trade has been redirected from Latin America to Canada and Asia, and finally we have become less reliant upon merchandise exports to finance our merchandise imports.

Notes

1. These figures, like others not otherwise referenced, are taken or computed from the United States Department of Commerce, *Survey of Current Business* (Washington: U.S. Government Printing Office).

2. *Economic Report of the President* (Washington: U.S. Government Printing Office, 1973), p. 131.

14

3. These merely illustrative figures were gleaned from current newspaper articles.

4. *Wall Street Journal*, April 17, 1973, p. 22.

5. The following analysis does not hold in those markets effectively restricted by quotas.

6. Frank A. Nemec, "The Changing World of Steel," remarks at the American Iron and Steel Institute Steel Industry Economics Seminar, Northern Illinois University, De Kalb, Illinois, April 4, 1973.

7. Some of this 260 percent is accounted for by price inflation, which presumably Mr. Nemec did not reckon into his estimate of 100 percent; but the 160 percent difference leaves ample room for price deflating.

8. *South Bend Tribune*, April 22, 1973, p. 8.

3 The Evolution of Trade with Japan

Patricia Hagan Kuwayama[1]
Federal Reserve Bank of New York

The Role of Japan in Overall U.S. Trade

We have all become aware of the dramatic growth of Japan's importance in our overall trade. While only about 4 percent of U.S. exports went to Japan in 1950, Japan constitutes 10 percent of our export market now, more than any other single country except Canada.[2] On the import side, the change has been truly astounding: Japan was the source of only 2 percent of United States imports in 1950, but supplied fully 16 percent of them in 1972. This change has occurred quite gradually over the last twenty or so years, reflecting the more rapid growth of our exports to, and even more strikingly, of our imports from Japan, than of our overall trade. But, even though these patterns have been in evidence over two decades, it was only in 1965 that they finally materialized in a reversal of the United States' traditional trade surplus with Japan. In the past few years, the bilateral deficit of our trade with Japan has reached a scale unprecedented for trade between any two countries—hitting $3.2 billion in 1971 and then growing to $4.1 billion the following year, as our 1972 imports from Japan exceeded $9 billion and our exports to Japan came to $5 billion. These changes have impressed themselves on us rather suddenly—more so than would have been the case had there not been a substantial lag in most Americans' awareness of the transformation that has been going on in the Japanese economy itself. Once it came, however, the recognition of Japan's importance hit hard. It may therefore be worth reminding ourselves that the change in the United States trading position is actually a quite general one. As Table 3-1 shows, since 1965, when the United States trade surplus began to decline decidedly, we went from a surplus of $5 billion to a deficit of nearly $7 billion in 1972. Between $3.5 and $4 billion of the change was with Japan, the largest deterioration of our balance with any single country. However, our trade balance with Europe (including the United Kingdom) shifted adversely by well over $3 billion in the same period, and with Canada by about $2.5 billion. Perhaps most interesting in terms of its implications for the future is that our trade balance with Africa and Asia *outside* Japan has shifted unfavorably more than $3 billion since 1965. Much of the change has been in the last few years, when the balance actually swung into

Table 3-1
United States Balance of Trade by Area
(Balance of payments basis; in millions of dollars)

	1960	1965	1971	1972
Balance of Trade with:				
All regions	4,906	4,942	−2,666	−6,816
United Kingdom	466	214	− 112	− 291
Western Europe	2,083	2,470	937	− 301
Eastern Europe	122	7	183	493
Canada	861	642	−1,693	−1,839
Other Western Hemisphere	−194	−122	318	170
Japan	225	−388	−3,208	−4,101
Australia, New Zealand and South Africa	407	623	555	140
Other Countries in Africa and Asia	794	1,682	354	−1,087

Source: U.S. Department of Commerce, *Survey of Current Business*, Vol. 41, November 1961; Vol. 46, November 1965; Vol. 53, April 1973.

deficit, and in trade with smaller Asian countries. The only major areas with whom our trade surplus grew in these years were Eastern Europe ($0.5 billion) and Latin America ($0.3 billion). Without, therefore, subscribing to the view that Japan is the United States' major trading problem—a view usually based on an analytically meaningless comparison of the size of the bilateral U.S.-Japanese deficit with the overall United States trade gap—there are a number of ways in which it is perhaps reasonable to see Japan as a mirror of the United States' own trade experience in the last decade or so. In this sense, an examination of the bilateral trading relationship may contribute valuable lessons for our overall situation—both by illuminating some of the dominant patterns of change that have occurred in recent past, and by suggesting some rather different "emerging patterns" of the future.

Changes in the Postwar Period

Perhaps the most striking way in which Japan's experience mirrors our own is Japan's fundamental shift from a situation in which it was plagued by repeated trade and payments deficits to one of chronic and ever-increasing surplus. This happened during the same period—the latter half of the 1960s—as the United States' transition from trade surplus to deficit. In both cases, the change had been long in the making and took the form of a steady differential between the growth rates of imports and of exports. But both countries, also, had become thoroughly accustomed to their historical trading positions and were slow to recognize the need to change economic institutions and policies oriented to the past rather than the present. I have treated this at length elsewhere[3] and believe it is worth noting again here that for exactly a century preceding the beginning, in 1968, of what we now see as an uninterrupted Japanese trade surplus, Japanese citizens and policymakers had lived under a balance-of-payments "ceiling." This "ceiling," which was regarded as the effective constraint on economic growth and affected almost every aspect of economic policy-making, took the form of a sharp dip into a trade deficit caused by surging requirements for crucial imports that accompanied each spurt of industrial activity.

Partly because of guidance by the Japanese government, the Japanese economy has undergone phenomenal growth and structural change during the postwar period. In the process it has increased its international competitiveness in a broad range of manufacturing industries and achieved competitiveness in some areas where it had none before. In the entire period from 1953, when the Japanese economy was more or less back on its feet following the devastation of World War II, to 1970, the average rate of increase of Japanese exports (measured in current prices) was slightly over 17 percent, while Japan's imports grew about 13 percent on average.

Our own trade with Japan has followed fairly closely the overall pattern of Japanese trade, the average growth of United States imports from Japan being about 20 percent in the same period, and the growth of our exports to Japan about 14 percent. The fact that the United States has always been Japan's leading trading partner[4] made it natural that Japanese producers looked to this market as the place to make some of their most spectacular gains. The United States share of Japan's imports has somewhat declined and our share of Japan's exports has somewhat increased since the 1950s; both proportions have been in the neighborhood of 30 percent since 1965.

The spectacular productivity advance by Japanese manufacturers is in part attributable to favorable overall price performance in Japan relative to competing Western countries, particularly in the latter half of the 1960s.[5] However, some of the most important reasons for Japan's success are not captured by these overall cost and price measures, which are mainly confined to increases in efficiency in the production of existing goods. Japan has occupied a strategic position in the "product cycle," being among the first "follower" countries to adopt sophisticated technologies developed in the United States and Europe. Japanese producers, on the basis of a very high rate of addition to their capital stock, have taken maximum advantage of this opportunity by shifting production into goods with fast growing international markets, by improving the quality of existing products, and by developing new commodities for marketing. Combined with a vigorous promotional effort, this has enabled Japan's exporters to carve out an increasing portion of the world's market for manufactures, including the market in the United States.

On the United States side, the growth in imports from Japan has been part of a general tendency toward increasingly "cosmopolitan" consumption of manufactured goods. To a large extent this change reflects initiatives taken on the supply side—that is, the large scale effort which producers in a number of countries, and most notably in Japan, have made to build up productive capacity and distribution networks specifically suited to servicing what they saw as potential markets in the United States and elsewhere. Almost all of the industrial countries of the world (although Japan has been a notable exception, a matter I will refer to again) have experienced increases in the proportions of their domestically consumed manufactures supplied from importing. The distinguishing characteristic of the United States' experience in this regard was that it participated in the trend primarily as an importer, but not very much as an exporter. Some other countries—for example, West Germany, Belgium, Italy, and Switzerland—added as much, or more, to their exports as they did to their imports, as the result of this worldwide growth of manufactures trade.[6] United States corporations have of course participated much more actively in the development of export markets than is indicated by their exports from geographical locations within the United States. The fact that United States' firms have responded to those opportunities to such a large extent by locating productive capacity overseas is one factor contributing to the unusual pattern of United States trade growth.

The Role of Japan's Government

American businessmen have complained, with some justification, that their Japanese counterparts enjoyed an advantage not available to themselves, in the sense that Japanese exports have had relatively free access to the American market—and much encouragement from their own government—at the same time that Japan's domestic market has been closed to foreign imports. The close and cooperative relationship between the large corporations and the government in Japan has received a great deal of attention in this country, and certainly the Japanese economic system does work differently from our own in many ways. Still, I think we need to temper our notion of "Japan, Inc." by reminding ourselves that Japan's is a market economy, and we would not have seen such impressive performance over the past twenty years had Japanese producers paid more attention to administrative guidance than to profit. Just as important, we need to realize how much Japanese commercial policy has changed in the past few years, in recognition—albeit more slowly than we might have wished—that the balance-of-payments deficit problem around which this policy was built is indeed a thing of the past.

First, let us examine policy on the export side. A number of programs have provided direct encouragement of exporting: The Bank of Japan offered short-term credits against export bills at preferential rates; the tax law included a number of provisions for exemption from or deferral of taxes and for rebate of import duties paid for inputs used to produce exports. All of these programs together are estimated to have saved exporters an amount equivalent to about 1 to 1.5 percent of the total value of their exported products, with more than half of this representing the deferral of tax payments, rather than 100 percent exemption from charges.[7] These programs were too small to be a primary reason for the Japanese export success story, though this of course does not mean that they were justified either. The bulk of the benefits that have accrued to exporters from preferential treatment were due to two programs, both of which have been eliminated within the last three years: namely, the accelerated depreciation provisions for exporting companies and the preferential credit facilities. In fact, the preferential export financing program has been replaced by a Bank of Japan facility for financing *imports* at preferential rates in order to stem the large once-and-for-all short-term capital inflow that could otherwise have followed the elimination of domestic export financing. Significantly, no one has suggested that this program has an important impact in encouraging imports. Direct government incentives for exporting thus are—or should be—a dead issue now, if they ever were very important.

Much more significant as a stimulus to exporting has been the Japanese government's "indicative planning," which has guided resources into the sectors of the economy regarded by the government as potential exporters. The effects of this policy are impossible to measure. They are also slow to be reversed, since this must be accomplished mainly through the allocation of new additions to capital. A change in direction is evident, however, as the government is now devoting more attention to the development of housing, sanitation, and other types of social "infrastructure," and to salvaging the already severely damaged environment of the Japanese islands. Some Japanese economists[8] have been extremely critical of the government for the tortoise-like pace at which it has carried out this reorientation, which has been emphasized in official Japanese economic plans for quite a number of years without having had an appreciable effect on the allocation of public spending until recently. But now, strongly reinforced by the appreciation of the yen as well as by long-term changes such as the rising expectations of Japanese workers and consumers and the closing of the "technology gap," the change in economic policy is bound to have an effect in slowing the phenomenal advance of Japanese manufacturing productivity.

On the import side, Japan's domestic market probably has been more protected against competition by foreign manufactures than that of any other industrialized country in the postwar period. Exporters to Japan have been discouraged by a complicated network of official and quasi-official regulations, which have seemed to extend to almost every major area of potential competition. This is undoubtedly one reason for the strikingly high concentration of Japanese imports in intermediate and capital goods as opposed to consumer goods. Only 5 to 6 percent of Japanese purchases from abroad were of non-food consumer goods (including passenger cars) in 1970,[9] in contrast with almost 30 percent for the United States.[10] The United States imports an unusually high proportion of consumer manufactures; still, Japan's percentage stands out as unusually low in comparison with almost all OECD countries.[11]

This situation of universal protection no longer really exists in Japan. It is worth devoting some attention to this here, since it is a matter in which foreign awareness seems once again to be lagging seriously behind Japanese reality. There are some reasons for this lag. One is the "credibility gap" which the Japanese government has created for itself since it first announced its "import liberalization" program in the early 1960s. Having acquired obligations to free imports by its acceptance of Article XI of GATT (in 1963), and of Article 8 of the IMF agreements and full membership in the OECD (in 1964), Japan responded to international pressure to carry out such liberalization—which it was not yet prepared to live with—by announcing one nominal liberalization measure after another, measures usually designed to have little perceptible effect on actual imports. After nearly a decade of this, it is not too surprising that many foreigners have failed to appreciate the really quite significant changes that have now finally occurred in the last few years.

Second, Japanese bureaucrats have had a tendency to retain the form of import-control regulations long after any substantive application has ceased. The law requiring import deposits, for instance, remained on the books until the end of 1972, presumably "in case" it should be needed again, even though a deposit ratio of zero percent has been applied since May 1970. Licenses are still required for all importing, and until 1972 a substantial number of items required approval from the Ministry of International Trade and Industry, though this approval was automatically granted. This overly cautious manner of carrying out reform has certainly contributed to foreign irritation, if not misunderstanding, over the true nature of Japanese commercial policy.[12]

The most important barrier has been import quotas. In 1968, Japan had 122 Brussels Tariff Nomenclature (BTN) items under what it calls "Residual Import Quotas" i.e., those to be removed eventually in compliance with GATT; of these fifty-four were industrial products and sixty-eight nonindustrial items. In addition, forty-odd BTN categories are affected by quotas for which Japan claims exemption under GATT. Most of these relate to military equipment or narcotics, but a few—rice and several other agricultural commodities, and perhaps some computer and aircraft items—can be considered protective of domestic industries. Taken all together, these quantitative restrictions covered a much broader range of commodities in Japan than was true of most other industrial countries, particularly in the area of non-agricultural products. The number of residual quotas is now down to thirty-two, including eight industrial products. The quotas which remain—those on agricultural items as well as industrial goods—do seem to be ones of particular importance to the United

Table 3-2

Japanese Import Quotas, 1962-72 (total number of 4-digit BTN categories subject to any quota restrictions)

	Unliberalized Import Items	Residual Import Quota Items	Of which:	
			Industrial Products	Agricultural[a] Products
April 1962	492	453	n.a.	n.a.
April 1965	162	123	n.a.	n.a.
April 1968	165	122	54	68
April 1969	163	120	52	68
October 1969	161	118	50	68
February 1970	152	109	45	64
April 1970	141	98	39	59
September 1970	133	90	35	55
January 1971	123	80	31	49
June 1971	103	60	20	40
September 1971	83	40	12	28
April 1972	76	33	9	24
April 1973	75	32	8	24

[a]Chapters 1 through 24 of the Brussels Tariff Nomenclature.

Sources: *Japan Foreign Trade News* (Tokyo: Boeki Koho-Sha), April 1970, December 1970, and February 1971; Leon Hollerman, *Japan's Dependence on the World Economy* (Princeton: Princeton University Press, 1967), p. 234 fn. 2; Japan Trade Center, *US-Japan News Digest* (New York, August 1972); U.S.-Japan Trade Council.

States, the most obvious case being the still-rigid restrictions on imports of computer items.

Aside from quotas, the import-deposit program was a general deterrent to importing in the 1960s. The rate has at times been as high as 10 percent for raw materials and 35 percent for consumer goods. But, as noted, this program has not been in effect since 1970.

Tariffs, which have now become much more important than they were in earlier years, when other barriers predominated, have also been significantly lowered. Before the Kennedy Round, Japanese tariffs were higher on average than those of most industrialized countries, and effective tariff protection was particularly high.[13] The Kennedy Round brought Japan's average tariff rate, measured as a simple average for all industrial BTN items, down to 10 percent. The 20 percent across-the-board cut effected in January 1973 lowered it again, to 8.5 percent, as compared with about 11 percent for the United States and 7 percent for the Economic Community.

Turning to less formal types of control, "administrative guidance" has discouraged large Japanese corporations, to an unknown degree, from purchasing intermediate and capital goods overseas, particularly in the early years when the Ministry of International Trade and Industry controlled foreign exchange allocations to all industries. As in all countries, some import-deterrents are also built into the domestic tax and regulatory structure. A famous example is the commodity tax on automobiles, which until 1973 was applied at a rate of 40 percent on large autos, and 15 percent on small cars. (The rate for large cars has now been reduced to 20 percent.)

The principal remaining case of all-around government protection is the computer industry. As it had done in the past with respect to steel, automobiles, and electronics, the Japanese government has now determined that it wishes to foster an internationally competitive computer industry in Japan, using all its traditional means—administrative guidance, preferential credit facilities, import quotas and high tariffs, direct investment restrictions, government purchasing guidelines and doubtless others as well. With the possible exception of aircraft and other defense-related industries which, being almost entirely under government purchase, do not require complex control networks for the same policy to be carried out, this does seem to be an isolated phenomenon among Japanese industries now. The changes in import quotas already noted, and my own investigations into recent changes in Japan's tariff structure,[14] show—with the single exception of computers—a clear tendency on the part of Japanese policy-makers to slash protective levels for modern industries like steel and automobiles, which were previously shielded as "infant" industries, but which have now outgrown that status. Liberalization of less competitive, traditional, labor-intensive industries proceeds more cautiously, but these areas presumably are not, with the possible exception of food products, of as much concern to American producers.

All of this seems to indicate that the United States is well-advised to continue pressing for more liberal Japanese policies in the areas that are of importance to us. At the same time, American producers in other industries should not be persuaded, by looking at these instances, that exporting to Japan is hopelessly blocked by a general official policy of protection against all types of foreign products, although such a belief might have been justified a few years ago.

Emerging Patterns of U.S.-Japanese Trade

Some patterns can be expected to emerge more strongly in coming years than in the past. In the "product cycle," we will see some of the industries that previously moved to Japan from the United States and Europe now moving from Japan to more labor-abundant countries. In textiles, electronics, and some steel processing industries, to mention a few, we have seen this pattern already, and it has almost certainly contributed to the change in our trade balance with smaller Asian countries that was noted at the beginning of this survey.

Another emerging pattern that we may see in coming years is that Japan will take more of the lead among industrial countries in advocating free-trade policies, a lead which for at least part of the postwar period has been taken by the United States. Japan's growing self-confidence in its ability to compete as a producer has diminished its fear of opening domestic markets. At the same time, the role of Japan as a prominent buyer of imports competing with the United States and other nations in important world markets has come more and more into focus as a source of potential conflicts. Both of these developments make it possible that Japan, more than most other industrial countries, will find it in its own best interest to push for a reciprocal movement toward free trade policies rather than protection in international forums.

What about the basic economic issues that have divided the United States and Japan in the past several years? Will we see a reversal of the United States' bilateral deficit with Japan, under the present set of exchange rates? I would say this is a reasonably likely prospect for the latter part of the decade—but not without hastening to add that I think that one of the lessons U.S.-Japanese trade has illustrated more effectively than any other is the difficulty of knowing what "equilibrium" exchange rates may be over any period of time or what they will bring to bilateral balances in a world where trade is large, structural change rapid, and national economic policy firmly committed to placing domestic objectives ahead of external considerations.

The 35 percent increase we have seen in the yen/dollar exchange rates has sharply curtailed Japanese producers' plans for exporting from Japan to the American market. This is leading them to pay increased attention to alternative markets and to opportunities for relocating production in the United States and third countries.

The currency realignment has surely also opened new possibilities for American exports in Japan. Still, selling in Japan remains a hard nut to crack, and it is difficult to predict how American firms will respond to these possibilities. The problem of distribution in Japan is not, I suspect, mainly one of monopoly by huge trading companies with strong loyalties to their *zaibatsu* connections among domestic producers. This comes back to the observation made above, that Japan's is, after all, a market system. *Zaibatsu* loyalties, at least in the postwar period, with the groups having lost much of their earlier economic cohesion, are always strongly tempered by an awareness of profit potential.[15] Some American exporters are finding that if the big trading companies do not handle their business, other Japanese firms will. Others are finding it advantageous to do their own retailing in Japan, although retailing activities by foreign firms are still subject to restrictions, of which the limitation of chainstore development is perhaps the most important.

In saying that penetration may be difficult, I am thinking mainly of such problems as language and the generally cumbersome system for distribution of goods in Japan, factors that may make it less congenial or promising than some other world markets for American exporters. A factor that may prove quite important is the changing attitude of the Japanese government toward producing activities by foreign corporations in Japan. The small role of the multinationals has been a distinguishing characteristic of United States dealings in Japan, as opposed to United States activity in other markets. This is certainly at least partially attributable to Japanese official policy, which has strongly discouraged foreign direct investments. Until quite recently, the Japanese authorities have apparently felt that any substantial participation by foreign enterprises might disturb the unique system of government-business relations under which the Japanese economy operates. As of May 1973, however, the government had effected a significant change in its policy. Rules governing foreign direct investments had been liberalized to allow unlimited investment, both in new and in established firms, in most manufacturing sectors. Not surprisingly, the computer industry is being excepted for the time being, along with some other manufacturing industries. Retail trade operations remain subject to case-by-case approval indefinitely, as do primary-producing, oil refining, and leather industries. While these exceptions are important, the new policy has removed governmental barriers to foreign entry in three-quarters of Japan's manufacturing industry, and this undoubtedly will mean some new opportunities for American producers to locate profitable operations in Japan. To the extent that American corporations are oriented to selling overseas mainly through manufacturing subsidiaries, this may increase the scope for future United States export development in Japan.

Even if the major countries refrain from defending any particular exchange rates against market trends, will this resolve the economic frictions between the United States and Japan? Not unless each country is willing to accept the changes in its external payments balance which currency realignment brings about. The adjustments will not be confined to trading relationships. Revaluation of the yen has also added to the existing incentives for Japanese firms to locate productive activities overseas at the same time that dollar devaluation has presumably reduced the attraction of foreign investment for American corporations relative to domestic investment. (The above-mentioned liberalization of Japanese policy toward investment by foreigners is an offsetting favorable influence on the growth of American investment in Japan, and the net effect of the two factors cannot easily be gauged.) Although a majority of Japanese foreign investments will probably continue to be concentrated in lower-wage countries in Asia, increasing amounts are finding their way to the United States in industries where production here has become a more advantageous way of servicing American markets than shipping from Japan. Whether or not this could result in a significant net flow of investment capital from Japan to the United States is far from obvious. As can be seen in Table 3-3, direct investments (in fact, all capital flows between Japan and the United States) have been completely dwarfed in magnitude by trade flows until now. Of course, if the balance-of-payments adjustment is accomplished partly through a flow of capital

Table 3-3

Current and Long-term Capital Transactions between the United States and Japan, 1960-72 (in billions of dollars)

	1960	1961	1962	1963	1964	1965	1966	1967	1968	1969	1970	1971	1972
American Exports to Japan	1.4	1.8	1.5	1.8	2.0	2.1	2.3	2.7	2.9	3.5	4.6	4.1	5.0
American Imports From Japan	-1.1	-1.1	-1.4	-1.5	-1.8	-2.4	-3.0	-3.0	-4.1	-4.9	-5.9	-7.3	-9.1
Balance of Trade	+0.2	+0.7	+0.2	+0.3	+0.2	-0.4	-0.6	-0.4	-1.1	-1.4	-1.2	-3.2	-4.1
Net Invisible Payments	-0.3	-0.2	-0.2	-0.2	-0.1	-0.1	-0.3	-0.2	-0.3	-0.4	-0.3	-0.3	-0.7
Balance on Current Account	-0.1	+0.5	0.0	+0.1	+0.1	-0.5	-0.9	-0.6	-1.4	-1.8	-1.5	-3.5	-4.8
U.S. Direct Investment in Japan	0.0	0.0	-0.1	-0.1	-0.1	0.0	0.0	0.0	-0.1	-0.1	-0.1	-0.2	-0.2
Japanese Direct Investment in U.S.	0.0	0.0	0.0	0.0	0.0	0.0	0.0	0.0	0.1	0.0	0.0	-0.5	0.1
Other Long-term Capital, Net	0.0	-0.1	-0.3	-0.4	-0.1	0.0	0.1	0.1	0.2	-0.2	0.1	-0.1	0.6
Basic Balance	-0.1	+0.3	-0.3	-0.3	-0.1	-0.5	-0.9	-0.5	1.2	-2.1	-1.6	-4.3	-4.3
Memorandum item:													
U.S. Current Military Expenditures in Japan	-0.4	-0.4	-0.4	-0.4	-0.3	-0.3	-0.5	-0.5	-0.6	-0.7	-0.7	-0.6	-0.8

Source: U.S. Department of Commerce, *Survey of Current Business*, Vols. 41-53, 1961-73.

toward the United States, then the trade adjustment implied by a given change in exchange rates may be made correspondingly smaller for the time being. (Eventually, of course, the income from direct investments must lead to a net flow of income in the opposite direction, i.e. toward the investing country.) All of these things are as much a part of the market mechanism which brings about equilibrium in international transactions as are changes in importing patterns, and there is no obvious reason why we should be concerned about the particular balance-of-payments structure they will create.

In the past, however, most countries—the United States and Japan clearly included—have tended to form rather specific preferences for the shape of their balance of payments "equilibria." Many of the conflicts that have divided the United States and Japan in the past several years have, in fact, stemmed from inconsistencies in such balance-of-payments aims. The United States, in its New Economic Policy of August 1971, and again in the statements surrounding the February 1973 devaluation, has expressed determination to recapture its old position of substantial overall trade surplus. Japan, on the other hand, has—implicitly in its economic plans since 1970, and explicitly since the summer of 1972—aimed at a current account surplus equivalent to 1 percent of its GNP, expecting this to be balanced by long-term capital outflows. This Japanese goal would have meant a substantial reduction from the surplus rates of the past few years, but would still, according to official Japanese projections, have implied a trade surplus on the order of $7 billion in 1975.[16] These goals are probably incompatible with one another, given other OECD countries' expectation of being in trade balance if not trade surplus—with the oil-producing countries and some of the other smaller nations looking forward to substantial surpluses, and with less developed countries generally desirous of limiting as much as possible their dependence on capital inflow by reducing their trade deficits.

Aside from the question of clinging to particular exchange rates, therefore, there will continue to be problems between the United States and Japan if both countries are not willing to accept the consequences in terms of changed expectations for their overall trade balances. There is no escape from the mathematical result that trade balances of all countries in the world must add to zero. Both the United States and Japan have shown reluctance to admit this, as have other countries as well. Both nations have seemed determined to set their own balance-of-payments targets in terms of domestic needs alone (though the "need" for a trade surplus is not proved in either case) without regard to implications for global equilibrium.

Notes

1. The views expressed here are my own, and are not to be attributed to the Federal Reserve Bank of New York.

2. Except where noted otherwise, trade statistics in this paper are from the U.S. Department of Commerce's *Survey of Current Business*, or the Bank of Japan's *Economic Statistics Annual* and *Economic Statistics Monthly*.

3. Patricia Kuwayama, "Japan's Balance of Payments and its Changing Role in the World Economy," in Jerome B. Cohen, ed., *Pacific Partnership* (Lexington, Mass.: Lexington Books, D.C. Heath and Company, 1972), pp. 51-79.

4. The 1930s and World War II years are an exception. In all other years since Japan was opened to international trade in the 1950s, the United States has had the largest share in its exports of any single country.

5. The decided advantage which the United States seemed to enjoy in terms of unit labor cost inflation in the first half of the decade—with respect to Japan as well as our European trading partners—was reversed in the 1965-70 period. Arthur Neef, "Unit Labor Costs in the United States and 10 Other Nations," *Monthly Labor Review*, vol. 95, July 1972, pp. 3-8. A similar pattern emerges on comparison of Japanese with American wholesale price increases, the Japanese price index flattening out in the same 1965-70 years when the United States was experiencing accelerated inflation. This comparison stands out particularly clearly when it is limited to larger establishments, the sector which produces most of the internationally competitive goods in Japan. Unpublished tables supplied by Dr. Eleanor Hadley.

6. William H. Branson and Helen B. Junz, "Trends in US Trade and Comparative Advantage," in *Brookings Papers on Economic Activity*, 1971-II, pp. 285-345.

7. Estimates of the tax benefits are based on unpublished tables supplied by Dr. Eleanor Hadley, and I have added my own rough estimate of the probable impact of preferential trade financing.

8. For one prominent example, see Hirofumi Uzawa, "Nihon keizai no kokusaiteki koritsu—Tsuka chosei no shindankai o megutte" ("Japan's Isolation in the International Arena over the New Stage of Currency Adjustment"), *Chuo Koron*, February 1972, pp. 102-119 (translation appearing in *Japanese Economic Studies*, vol. 1, Fall 1972, pp. 7-30).

9. Japan Tariff Commission, *Summary Report Trade of Japan*, December 1970, Table 4 and 5, pp. 67 ff.

10. *Survey of Current Business*, June 1972, p. 40.

11. Kathryn Morisse, "Trade Data of OECD Countries by End-Use Commodity Categories" (unpublished discussion paper, 1971).

12. For an excellent discussion of this and other aspects of Japan's nontariff barriers, see Kiyoshi Kojima, "Nontariff Barriers to Japan's Trade," *Hitotsubashi Journal of Economics*, vol. 13, June 1972, pp. 1-39.

13. Patricia Kuwayama, "The Effective Protection of Japanese Manufacturing Industries," (Ph.D. dissertation, City University of New York, 1970).

14. Patricia Kuwayama, "Tariff Protection and Japanese Industry" (unpublished).

15. Eleanor Hadley, *Antitrust in Japan* (Princeton: Princeton University Press, 1970), Chapter 18.

16. Report of statement by MITI official Yugoro Komatsu in the *Financial Times*, London, September 7, 1972.

4

Emerging U.S. Trade Patterns with Western European Countries

George Rich
Carleton University

Introduction

President Nixon's trade bill is a clear indication of growing United States dissatisfaction with the world trade patterns that have emerged in recent years. Despite the gradual lowering of barriers to trade since the end of World War II, the United States claims to be the principal victim of the new preferential trading arrangements that have evolved in Western Europe. American frustrations are exacerbated by the fact that the United States government has been a key driving force behind the movement toward free trade.

In this chapter our attention will be focused on the trade relations between the United States and Western Europe. The study will be divided into three parts. First, we shall examine the evolution of postwar trade relations in order to identify the principal bones of contention between the United States and Western Europe. Second, we shall analyze the impact on trade flows of Western European integration. Third, we shall explore briefly the possibilities of resolving the conflicts between the United States and Western Europe.

Evolution of the Trade Relations Between the United States and Western Europe

At the end of World War II, there was a widespread feeling that the nationalist and protectionist policies of the 1930s had to be abandoned if rapid reconstruction of the wartorn economies was to be achieved. Trade liberalization, in turn, proceeded along two avenues: European economic integration and multilateral tariff negotiations under the auspices of the GATT.

European Economic Integration

The Economic Commission for Europe (ECE), established in 1947 as a regional agency of the United Nations, the Organization for European Economic Cooperation (OEEC), and the Council of Europe were the results of early efforts to develop economic cooperation among the nations of Europe. The OEEC was created on the initiative of the United States, which was reluctant to accept sole responsibility for the distribution of Marshall Aid and wanted this task to be assigned to an international organization. In addition, the members of the OEEC agreed to eliminate quotas and to liberalize payments on a mutual basis. Although the OEEC largely met its objectives, it was unable to resolve a fundamental conflict between Britain and certain other members.[1] Britain argued that decisions should be taken only by unanimous vote. A group of members led by France took the opposite point of view and opted for an organization endowed with supranational powers. The French considered the OEEC to be the first step towards political as well as economic union. Although they agreed that integration would be associated with significant economic gains, they placed even more emphasis on the political aims of European unification. The British, on the other hand, showed little interest in the political aspects of integration as the Commonwealth, rather than Europe, formed their frame of reference.

Since the French point of view did not prevail, the nations favoring a supranational approach to integration were left with no other choice but to realize their plans outside the framework of OEEC. After several projects for political unification had failed, these efforts finally came to fruition with the establishment in 1958 of the European Economic Community. Although the EEC was concerned primarily with economic matters, its members hoped that economic integration would pave the way for political unification. Within the EEC, the international movement of goods, capital, labor, and enterprises was to be liberalized. National tariffs were to be replaced by a common external tariff. Internal tariffs were to be eliminated gradually by December 31, 1969. It was also agreed to frame a set of common policies dealing with nontariff barriers to trade, agriculture, transport, energy, regional economic development, social security, macro-stabilization, monetary matters, industrial structure, and external relations. Three supranational bodies were entrusted with the implementation of these policies: The Council of Ministers, the Commission, and the Court of Justice. Initially, voting in the Council was to be based on a unanimity rule; but eventually decisions would be taken by majority vote.[2]

At this stage the United States was a strong supporter of European integration.[3] United States attitudes towards the EEC reflected largely political and military considerations. It was felt that economic and political unification of Europe would strengthen the Atlantic Alliance. For this reason, the United States was opposed to any modification of the Rome Treaty through the establishment of a free trade area embracing the EEC as well as other Western European nations. On the initiative of Britain, negotiations for a Europe-wide free trade area started in 1957. However, since the Six were suspicious of Britain's intentions, these negotiations ended in failure.

It is well known that Britain's efforts eventually resulted in the establishment of a truncated European Free Trade Association (EFTA). The purpose of the EFTA arrangement was to establish free trade in industrial goods. The members did not adopt a common external tariff, nor did they attempt to harmonize their economic policies. Since the agreement did not extend to trade in agricultural products, Britain could continue to rely on her traditional cheap sources of food supply. Internal tariffs were eliminated rapidly and complete liberalization of trade was achieved by the end of 1966.

However, the division of Western Europe into two trade blocs was not to last long. Britain realized that she would face growing isolation if she did not seek membership in the EEC. The lengthy and tortuous negotiations, as well as the two French vetos, have been described elsewhere and need not concern us here. However, it may be useful to give a brief description of the final terms of the agreement between the EEC and Britain.[4] There is a five-year transition period which started on January 1, 1973. During the transition period, tariffs on trade between Britain and the other members of the EEC will be gradually eliminated. Moreover, Britain will, in a number of stages, adopt the common external tariff and the common agricultural policy (CAP). Britain has also agreed to make a gradually increasing contribution to the Community budget. After 1980 Community budgetary finance will become applicable to Britain, i.e., 90 percent of levies and customs duties will accrue to the Community budget, as well as up to 1 percent of the revenue from the value-added tax. Special provisions have been made for British dairy imports from New Zealand and sugar imports from the Caribbean islands.

EFTA will continue as a separate organization, although most of its members have either joined the EEC or have negotiated free trade agreements with the Community. However, the EFTA members who decided against membership in the EEC have only been offered industrial free trade; they will not participate in the common agricultural policy. Moreover, with the exception of antitrust, the free trade agreements do not entail any coordination or harmonization of economic policy.

The EEC has also sought to establish closer trade links with the nations of Southern Europe and Africa. Over the years, it has built a fragile edifice known as the Mediterranean policy. With the exception of Albania, Lybia, and Syria, all the Mediterranean nations have negotiated or are in the process of negotiating (Cyprus, Algeria) trade agreements with the EEC.[5] In most of these agreements the Mediterranean nations are accorded preferential treatment for their exports to the EEC. These nations in return have agreed to cut their tariffs on their imports of industrial products from the EEC (reverse preferences). In addition, the EEC has recently advanced a bold scheme which would entail negotiating free trade agreements with each Mediterranean country. As I shall show later, these plans have met stiff opposition from the United States and are therefore unlikely to get very far.[6] However, the continued efforts by the EEC to extend the southern boundary of the European preferential trading area clearly indicate that it considers the Mediterranean to be its preserve.

The shifts in trade patterns resulting from the rapid growth of the European preferential trading area have become a major concern of the United States. As we pointed out, United States support of European integration was originally based on the assumption that a unified Europe would foster the Atlantic Alliance. This assumption did not prove to be entirely correct as substantial conflicts of interest emerged between the United States and several Western European countries. The widening gulf between the Atlantic partners led to a reassessment on the part of the United States of its policy towards Europe. The United States was not prepared to tolerate excessive European discrimination against her exports and sought refuge in multilateral trade negotiations within the framework of GATT.

Multilateral Tariff Negotiations

The General Agreement on Tariffs and Trade (GATT) has made an important contribution to trade liberalization in the postwar period.[7] The members of GATT have agreed to deal with each other on a non-discriminatory basis. Preferential trading areas are to be tolerated only if they result, or are expected to result, in free trade within the area. Since the GATT's emphasis is on worldwide liberalization of trade, it constitutes a useful counterweight to the efforts for regional integration.

Between 1947 and 1961 the GATT launched five rounds of tariff negotiations which led to a significant reduction in trade barriers. It is interesting to note that in the early years of GATT most continental European countries were dissatisfied with the slow pace at which the negotiations were progressing. However, attempts to speed up trade liberalization were frustrated by the United States and Britain. The reluctance of the two major trading nations to stage a full-scale attack on trade barriers provided a strong impetus to the continental European nations to pursue further liberalization within the framework of regional arrangements.[8] To an increasing extent, the Americans were confronted with trade blocs that tended to discriminate against United States exports.

As a result of these developments, the United States sought to reactivate the GATT machinery to extract concessions from the EEC. The Kennedy administration embarked on a new bold venture designed to dismantle trade barriers. Under the Trade Expansion Act of 1962, the President was authorized to cut tariffs by 50 percent and to eliminate duties on free-world export products of which at least 80 percent are accounted for by the United States and the EEC. The Kennedy Round of tariff negotiations was successfully completed in 1967. It resulted in significant tariff cuts despite the fact that the 80 percent clause became ineffective when Britain failed to gain admission to the EEC. The average tariff on imports of finished manufactures now amounts to only 7.2 to 12.0 percent in the United States, 7.8 to 8.7 percent in the EEC, and 8.2 to 11.3 percent in the United Kingdom, depending on the method of calculating the averages.[9] However, the Kennedy Round negotiations were less successful in other respects. They did not effectively deal with the problem of agricultural protection, nor did they come to grips with the complex question of the nontariff barriers to trade. The negotiations with regard to agriculture are of particular interest and will be discussed very briefly.

Since the United States is a major exporter of agricultural products, the Kennedy administration insisted that agriculture be part of a bargain on tariffs. The EEC was very reluctant to offer concessions on the agricultural front, as this could not have been accomplished without major modifications of its common agricultural policy. CAP is a complex machinery of protection which was thrashed out during a series of tortuous bargaining sessions. The negotiations were accompanied by a major clash over financing the support program, which caused the French to withdraw from the Community between July 1965 and January 1966. CAP is based on a system of price supports for a wide range of commodities. Prices are maintained through (1) official support buying and (2) a system of variable import levies and export subsidies designed to insulate the domestic markets from the fluctuations in the world prices. The levies (subsidies) are adjusted automatically when the foreign prices of imports (exports) change relative to the domestic prices. Consequently, liberalization of agricultural trade between the EEC partners and nonmembers can be achieved only through a modification of the Community's price support policies.

Despite heavy United States pressure, the EEC refused to consider a major overhaul of CAP. It was not prepared to reopen a debate which had almost destroyed the Community. To avert a collapse of the negotiations, the United States government softened its stand on agriculture. Thus the Kennedy Round did not result in a significant liberalization of trade in agricultural products.[10]

After the completion of the negotiations, the United States government realized that the Kennedy Round had weakened its bargaining position considerably. Since the barriers inhibiting agricultural trade had not been dismantled, the United States did not appear to benefit as much from the tariff negotiations as the Western European countries and Japan. The bulwark protecting European agriculture seemed to be impregnable. The EEC could not be persuaded to modify CAP or the Mediterranean policy because, as a result of the tariff cuts, the United States was no longer able to grant significant concessions on the industrial front. To strengthen the United States bargaining position, President Nixon introduced a set of new international commercial policies in August 1971. Professor Curzon has argued[11] that Nixon's economic measures must be viewed as a desperate attempt to shift the balance of power in favor of the United States, rather than as an expression of genuine protectionist sentiment. So far the President's initiative has been more successful in the balance of payments than in the trade area. However, the United States has been able to persuade her trade partners to embark on a new round of multilateral negotiations within the framework of GATT. In these negotiations the United States hopes to extract major trade concessions from the EEC and other industrialized nations.

Our historical survey suggests that the Kennedy Round tariff negotiations were only partially successful in alleviating the discriminatory aspects of European integration. Thus the trade effects of European integration are likely to loom large in the coming GATT round. In the following sections, I would like to discuss the quantitative importance of these problems and their possible solutions.

The Impact of European Integration on U.S. Trade

Trade Creation and Trade Diversion

The effect of European integration on trade patterns is commonly analyzed under the headings of trade creation and trade diversion.[12] Trade creation occurs if, as a result of the formation of a preferential trading area, production of a particular commodity is shifted from a high-cost domestic source to a low-cost supplier in a partner country. Trade diversion occurs if a high-cost source of supply in a partner country is substituted for a low-cost source in a nonmember country. Trade diversion is undesirable, as it may be associated with a loss in the real income of the partner and nonmember countries.

Thus the question arises whether European integration has resulted in extensive trade diversion. If a shift in trade from nonmember to partner countries could be observed, United States concern about the trade-pattern effects of European integration would be justified.

Table 4-1 provides a summary of the shifts in the structure of United States

Table 4-1
U.S. Trade: All Sectors (millions of dollars)

	Exports			Imports		
	EEC	EFTA	Total	EEC	EFTA	Total
1960-62 Average	3496	2044	20762	2306	1621	15086
percent	16.8	9.8	100.0	15.3	10.7	100.0
1969-71 Average	7600	3883	41177	6644	3784	40535
percent	18.5	9.4	100.0	16.4	9.3	100.0
Percent increase	117.4	90.2	98.3	188.1	133.4	168.7

Source: OECD, *Statistics of Foreign Trade*, Series B.

trade between 1960-62 and 1969-71. While the EEC has increased its share in total United States trade, a decrease can be observed for EFTA. Thus these figures do not point to extensive Western European discrimination against United States trade, at least not in the case of the EEC. Unfortunately, an examination of the actual changes in trade shares does not allow us to identify integration-induced changes in United States trade patterns. To remedy this deficiency, it is useful to employ a method, or variant of a method, which was developed by Balassa.[13] A preferential trading area is said to result in trade creation if, *ceteris paribus*, the members' total imports rise. Similarly, a reduction in imports from nonmembers provides evidence of trade diversion. Moreover, a customs union, in particular, could result in external trade creation if the adoption of the common external tariff were associated with a reduction in the degree of effective protection against outsiders. A rise in imports from nonmembers would indicate external trade creation.

Thus it is necessary to identify the changes in the member countries' total imports, as well as imports from nonmembers, attributable to the formation of a preferential trading area. This task can be accomplished in two ways: First, we can abstract from the influence on imports of changes in GNP, exchange rates, and similar factors, and assume that the residual reflects integration. Second, we can attempt to measure directly the impact of integration. Since the bulk of the studies cover only trade in manufactures,[14] we shall consider separately manufacturing and agriculture.

Manufacturing. The most comprehensive studies on this subject have been published by EFTA.[15] The most recent investigation covers trade in manufactures as well as certain raw materials and employs a residual method.[16] The results suggest that trade creation has outweighed diversion in both the EEC and EFTA. The establishment of EFTA has entailed relatively more trade diversion than the EEC, although for United States trade the opposite conclusion must be reached. The formation of the EEC resulted in a loss in United States manufacturing exports of $251 million in 1967 (or 7.8 percent of actual EEC imports from the United States), while EFTA accounted for a loss of $95 million (8.9 percent).[17]

Another estimate of the incidence of trade creation and diversion has been submitted by Truman.[18] Although the methodology underlying the EFTA and Truman studies are very similar, Truman's calculations reveal extensive external trade creation. He finds that in 1968 the United States suffered a loss of $240 million worth of exports to the EEC, but gained $423 million worth of exports to EFTA as a result of integration.[19] The EFTA figure seems to be implausible and is probably due to certain assumptions underlying his study.[20] However, as Clavaux[21] has pointed out, it is reasonable to conclude that European integration has not been accompanied by extensive trade diversion in manufactures because its discriminatory effects have been partly offset by the substantial efforts for trade liberalization on other fronts (OEEC, dollar liberalization, unilateral tariff reductions).

Krause[22] employs a direct method of estimating the impact of European integration on United States trade. He draws a distinction between the income and trade-pattern effects of integration, but we will focus on the trade-pattern effects. Krause's study suggests that the United States lost $273 million worth of exports to the EEC and $100 million to EFTA[23] as a result of the trade-pattern effects of integration. These figures are surprisingly close to the estimates submitted in the EFTA study.

Thus it appears that European integration has not seriously hurt United States trade in manufactures. All the studies report extensive trade creation, while trade diversion has assumed only modest proportions.

Agriculture. Tables 4-2 and 4-3 provide data on EEC and EFTA food imports from various sources. For the EEC we can observe a drastic reduction in the nonmembers' shares in total imports between 1960 and 1971. The United States share rose between 1960 and 1966, but declined gradually afterwards. On the whole, the United States has fared relatively better than other nonmembers, such as Canada, which seem to have borne the brunt of the EEC's discriminatory agricultural policies. However, as explained earlier, the changes in the nonmembers' shares in total imports are not a good indicator of the incidence of trade diversion. To arrive at a more satisfactory estimate, it is necessary to determine (1) the change in the nonmembers' shares in total EEC consumption of food products[24] and (2) the difference between the actual shares and a set of hypothetical figures excluding the integration effects. It is, of course, difficult to ascertain the pattern of shares that would have emerged in the absence of integration. A comparison of the EEC and EFTA experience might shed some light on this problem, because the EFTA agreement does not cover trade in agricultural products.

A glance at Table 4-3 suggests that the nonmembers, by and large, were able to maintain their 1960 share in total EFTA imports. However, if imports are related to total EFTA consumption (Table 4-4), we make the rather surprising discovery that the nonmembers' share fell substantially. For example, in 1970 the United States could have gained an additional $220 million worth of exports (or about 55 percent of the actual figure) to the EFTA countries if she had been able to maintain her 1960-62 share in total EFTA demand. Moreover, similar tendencies may be observed for the share of total imports in food consumption. Thus the evidence suggests that the EFTA countries have promoted their self-sufficiency in agricultural commodities at the expense of the producers in the other member nations and nonmember nations.

If we contrast the EFTA experience with the EEC data reported in Table 4-4, we find that the aggregate nonmember shares and the Canadian share fell somewhat between 1960-62 and 1968-70, while the United States share did not

Table 4-2
Source of EEC Food Imports, 1960-71 (millions of dollars)

	Food and Live Animals (S.I.T.C. Section Zero)					
Year	World	EEC	Outside Area	EFTA (excluding Finland, Iceland)	Canada	U.S.
1960	4860	1192	3668	481	133	438
1961	5049	1302	3747	478	167	580
1962	5811	1467	4344	524	143	710
1963	6352	1672	4680	623	150	738
1964	6988	1921	5067	631	138	820
1965	8028	2388	5640	681	153	996
1966	8469	2554	5915	642	162	1126
1967	8525	2814	5711	663	150	872
1968	9017	3406	5611	591	128	919
1969	10511	4471	6040	635	123	861
1970	11843	4983	6860	690	206	1093
1971	13312	5933	7379	730	236	1133
	Percent					
1960	100.0	24.5	75.5	9.9	2.7	9.0
1961	100.0	25.8	74.2	9.5	3.3	11.5
1962	100.0	25.2	74.8	9.0	2.5	12.2
1963	100.0	26.3	73.7	9.8	2.4	11.6
1964	100.0	27.5	72.5	9.0	2.0	11.7
1965	100.0	29.7	70.3	8.5	1.9	12.4
1966	100.0	30.2	69.8	7.6	1.9	13.3
1967	100.0	33.0	67.0	7.8	1.8	10.2
1968	100.0	37.8	62.2	6.6	1.4	10.2
1969	100.0	42.5	57.5	6.0	1.2	8.2
1970	100.0	42.1	57.9	5.8	1.7	9.2
1971	100.0	44.6	55.4	5.5	1.8	8.5

Source: OECD, *Statistics of Foreign Trade*, Series B and C.

change appreciably. Thus the nonmember producers have encountered fewer obstacles in the EEC than in the EFTA agricultural markets. Moreover, there has been a significant increase in intra-EEC trade, as indicated by the rise in the share of total imports in EEC consumption. In other words, while the degree of self-sufficiency in agricultural products of the Common Market as a whole has increased, the individual members have strengthened their dependence upon each other.

Table 4-3
Source of EFTA Food Imports, 1960-71 (millions of dollars)

Year	World	EFTA[a] (excluding Finland, Iceland)	Outside Area	EEC	Canada	U.S.
		Food and Live Animals (S.I.T.C. Section Zero)				
1960	5176	549	4627	612	328	468
1961	4946	549	4397	645	276	387
1962	5435	607	4828	681	312	526
1963	5755	677	5078	739	337	432
1964	6227	766	5461	809	368	500
1965	6189	805	5384	884	357	468
1966	6349	866	5483	898	310	559
1967	6326	870	5456	960	301	435
1968	5933	831	5102	934	259	364
1969	6150	850	5300	940	264	348
1970	6776	939	5837	1031	305	484
1971	7318	1046	6272	1170	344	509
		Percent				
1960	100.0	10.6	89.4	11.8	6.3	9.0
1961	100.0	11.1	88.9	13.0	5.6	7.8
1962	100.0	11.2	88.8	12.5	5.7	9.7
1963	100.0	11.8	88.2	12.8	5.9	7.5
1964	100.0	12.3	87.7	13.0	5.9	8.0
1965	100.0	13.0	87.0	14.3	5.8	7.6
1966	100.0	13.6	86.3	14.1	4.9	8.8
1967	100.0	13.8	86.2	15.2	4.8	6.9
1968	100.0	14.0	86.0	15.7	4.4	6.1
1969	100.0	13.8	86.2	15.3	4.3	5.7
1970	100.0	13.9	86.1	15.2	4.5	7.1
1971	100.0	14.3	85.7	16.0	4.7	7.0

[a]EFTA: United Kingdom, Norway, Sweden, Denmark, Austria, Switzerland, Portugal; excludes Finland and Iceland which joined EFTA in 1969 and 1970 respectively. This allows earlier and later years to be compared for the same area. The 1970 figures for imports from EFTA and Canada are estimates because Series C was not available for that year.
Source: OECD, *Statistics of Foreign Trade*, Series B and C.

The evidence lends support to the view that the integration of the EEC agricultural markets has not resulted in significant trade diversion. Given the dismal record of EFTA, it is likely that the nonmember share in total EEC consumption would have declined even more if CAP had not been formed.

Table 4-4
Imports as a Percentage of Total Food Consumption[a]

Year	All Sources	Imports from Outside Area	U.S.	Canada
		EEC		
1960-62	11.8	8.8	1.3	1.0
1968-70	13.8	8.2	1.3	0.6
		EFTA (excluding Finland, Iceland)		
1960-62	24.0	21.4	2.1	1.4
1968-70	21.3	18.3	1.4	0.9
		United Kingdom		
1960-62	21.1	18.8	1.6	1.4
1968-70	18.4	16.1	1.1	1.0

[a]All figures are expressed in current prices and exchange rates. Due to gaps in the statistics, only Finnish food consumption could be deducted from the total EFTA figures. To convert the figures for Finnish and British consumption into dollars, the following exchange rates were used: 1960-62: $0.3125, $2.80; 1968-70: $0.2381, $2.40.

Sources: OECD, *Statistics of Foreign Trade*, Series B and C; OECD, *National Accounts of OECD Countries*, 1960-70, pp. 30, 36, 138 and 316.

These conclusions, admittedly, are based on very crude calculations.[25] Disaggregation of the import figures would probably reveal a slightly different picture. CAP appears to have had a detrimental effect on imports of commodities that are subject to variable levies. For this reason, imports of U.S. cereals have grown less than total EEC food consumption. On the other hand, the United States has improved her export performance in animal foodstuffs, which are accorded liberal treatment by the EEC.[26] Moreover, the analysis fails to take into account the effect of export subsidies on trade flows. On the whole, however, it is safe to argue that the trade diversion effects of CAP have been modest compared with the protectionism prevalent in the EFTA cohort. As indicated by Table 4-4, even liberal-minded Britain has gradually enhanced her self-sufficiency in agricultural products in recent years. If the American share in total United Kingdom demand for food had remained at the 1960-62 level, the United States would have gained an additional $125 million worth of exports to the United Kingdom (or about 50 percent of the actual figure). It is interesting to note that the Canadian export performance in the British markets has been as bleak as that of the United States, despite the close Commonwealth ties. The British government is partly responsible for this situation, as it has sought to reduce the nation's dependence upon food imports for balance of payments reasons.[27] The evidence, therefore, does not lend support to the widespread belief that European integration has exacerbated agricultural protectionism. One might well venture the suggestion that CAP has tended to restrain the protectionist forces in member countries, such as Germany, which were known to support their farmers generously. Although the common prices set under CAP were on the average higher than the former national prices, the highly protectionist countries had to accept price cuts in many instances.[28] Nonetheless, the EEC can hardly be commended on its agricultural policies, which seem to perpetuate an ingrained European tradition of promoting self-sufficiency in agricultural products in order to assist the farmers.

Strategies for the GATT Negotiations

Although the trade-diversion effects of European integration have not been excessive, there is clearly room for further liberalization of trade between the United States and Western Europe, especially in the agricultural sector. The United States proposal for a new round of GATT negotiations spurred a reticent EEC into new action. It may be useful to discuss briefly the posture assumed by the two powers.

The United States has developed a reasonably coherent strategy with regard to the tariff negotiations. The official United States position seems to be embodied in two reports: the Williams Report submitted to President Nixon in 1971,[29] and the Rey Report prepared by the OECD.[30] The United States had made the rather remarkable proposal that all the tariffs on manufacturing products should be reduced to zero. Moreover, the United States wants significant concessions from the EEC on the agricultural front. A comprehensive review of all the nontariff barriers to trade is also proposed.

The EEC appears to have unearthed a suggestion that it advanced during the Kennedy Round negotiations. The Community claims that the negotiations should aim at a uniform level of industrial tariffs, not zero tariffs. This proposal is not acceptable to the American government, since it would affect primarily countries such as the United States which still maintain a small number of very high tariffs. On the other hand, the zero-tariff suggestion has fallen on deaf ears in the EEC. As Curzon[31] points out, the common external tariff is still the principal unifying element in the Common Market. Needless to say, the EEC has made only vague promises on agriculture and the preferential trade agreements with the developing countries. In the agricultural area the EEC is willing to negotiate international commodity agreements and rules on export subsidies (despite the fact that the International Wheat Agreement turned out to be an utter failure). However, the Community is not prepared to discuss the fundamental premises underlying CAP. Both EEC and American officials agree on the need to tackle the nontariff barriers to trade.

Thus, on most issues, there appears to exist a wide gulf between the views of the United States and the EEC. It will not be an easy task to resolve the conflicts between the two trade partners, for a number of reasons.

First, it is doubtful that a complete elimination of the industrial tariffs in the United States and Western Europe would result in significant income gains. On the whole, the existing American and Western European industrial tariffs cannot be considered serious impediments to international trade. Nor can it be argued that Western European integration has led to extensive diversion of trade in manufactures. Moreover, it would be impossible to reach the zero-tariff aim without a number of safeguards designed to protect industries hurt seriously by imports. These safeguards would, in many instances, violate the spirit of GATT and call for major modifications in it. Any relaxation of the GATT rules could only be detrimental to the free-trade case, as it would invite experimentation with new restrictive practices.

Thus a full-scale attack on industrial tariffs is not likely to result in substantial benefits. A second alternative appears to be more promising. The negotiations should review those sectors in which the governments have retained a high degree of protection. The reviews, of course, would have to cover tariff as well as nontariff obstacles to trade.[32] Our analysis suggests that in such sectors as agriculture significant income gains could be reaped if the various impediments to trade were dismantled. As we have seen, an effective liberalization of agricultural trade could be achieved only if the national and Community support policies were modified and harmonized. Thus the negotiations would have to address themselves to the complex question of policy harmonization.

There is little evidence suggesting that, at this point, the governments are ready to tackle the problem of policy harmonization. From the Rey Report[33] one gains a clear impression of the diversity of views expressed by the various governments on the problem of agricultural protection. Nonetheless, the United States should actively pursue the goal of freer trade in agricultural products. Although the negotiations are unlikely to yield significant results in the short run, the chances for a satisfactory agreement are better in the long run, as the Europeans themselves are beginning to search for alternative approaches to agricultural policy in order to curb the rapidly increasing cost of their price support programs. Moreover, our analysis suggests that the United States government should not attempt to undermine CAP, because it cannot be considered the principal obstacle to an expansion of United States agricultural trade. On the contrary, the existence of CAP is likely to facilitate the task of harmonization as it reduces the number of independent actors in the commercial policy field.

Summary and Conclusions

In this chapter we have discussed a number of problems that have marred the trade relations between the United States and Western Europe. The first part analyzed the evolution of the trade relations in the postwar period in order to identify the principal points at issue. Although the United States government has been a strong supporter of European integration, it has become increasingly concerned about the discriminatory aspects of EEC and EFTA commercial policies. To mitigate the effect on United States trade of European integration, the United States has relied heavily on tariff negotiations within the framework of GATT. The results of these negotiations have not been entirely satisfactory to the United States, as they have not resulted in a significant liberalization of agricultural trade.

The second part of the chapter provided a quantitative assessment of the trade-diversion effects of European integration. We found that diversion of trade in manufactures has been modest, while United States dissatisfaction with agricultural trade appears to be justified. However, our analysis does not lend support to the view that the EEC's common agricultural policy has been the principal culprit behind the disappointing performance of United States exporters in the European agricultural markets.

In the last section we discussed the prospects for further trade liberalization. We argued that the benefits associated with a complete elimination of industrial tariffs, as proposed by the United States, are *not* likely to be substantial, while a significant liberalization of agricultural trade would be desirable. However, the negotiations on agricultural trade are bound to progress slowly, for they must address themselves to the complex question of policy harmonization.

Notes

1. On this point see Dennis Swann, *The Economics of the Common Market*, 2nd ed. (Harmondsworth: Penguin Books, 1972), pp. 17-19.

2. During the agricultural crisis of 1965, the French President proposed that the Rome Treaty be amended to rule out majority voting. Although the Treaty was not changed, the Five had to accept a compromise solution. "As a result, where a country's vital national interest is at stake the majority voting system will not be used. This has been attractive to British politicians and was reaffirmed at the Pompidou-Heath 'summit' of 1971," ibid., p. 91.

3. See Lawrence B. Krause, *European Economic Integration and the United States* (Washington: The Brookings Institution, 1968), pp. 25-31.

4. The agreement is included in *The United Kingdom and the European Communities*, Cmnd. 4715 (London: HMSO, July 1971). For a brief summary of the agreement see Swann, op. cit., pp. 190-96.

5. These agreements take a variety of forms. Some countries (Greece, Turkey, Morocco, Tunisia, Malta) have concluded preferential agreements with the EEC. Agreements covering a limited range of products and moderate tariff reductions are in existence between the EEC and Spain, Israel, Egypt, the Lebanon, and Yugoslavia. Portugal, as a member of EFTA, concluded a free trade agreement. See John Lambert, "The Cheshire Cat and the Pond: EEC and

the Mediterranean Area," *Journal of Common Market Studies*, vol. 10, September 1971, pp. 37-46, and *The Economist*, vol. 248, August 12, 1972, p. 66.

6. *The Economist*, vol. 248, November 11, 1972, pp. 95-96.

7. For an excellent analysis of the GATT inspired negotiations see Robert E. Baldwin, "Toward the Next Round of Trade Negotiations," in Bela Belassa, ed., *Changing Patterns in Foreign Trade and Payments*, rev. ed. (New York: W.W. Norton, 1970), pp. 27-38, and Gerard and Victoria Curzon, "Options after the Kennedy Round," in Harry G. Johnson, ed., *New Trade Strategy for the World Economy* (Toronto and Buffalo: University of Toronto Press, 1969), pp. 20-73.

8. Baldwin, op. cit., pp. 30-32.

9. OECD, *Policy Perspectives for International Trade and Economic Relations*, Report by the High Level Group on Trade and Related Problems to the Secretary General of OECD (Paris: OECD, 1972), p. 162.

10. On this point see Thomas B. Curtis and John R. Vastine, Jr., *The Kennedy Round and the Future of American Trade*, Praeger Special Studies in International Economics and Development (New York and London: Praeger, 1971), pp. 26-40.

11. At a seminar given at Carleton University in November 1971.

12. These terms were first introduced by Jacob Viner, *The Customs Union Issue* (New York: Carnegie Endowment for International Peace, 1950), pp. 42-43.

13. See Bela Balassa, "Trade Creation and Trade Diversion in the European Common Market," *Economic Journal*, vol. 77, March 1967, pp. 1-21. In this chapter we do not provide a comprehensive survey of the studies on the trade-pattern effects of integration as this task has been performed elsewhere: Bela Balassa, op. cit.; Petrus J. Verdoorn and C.A. Bochove, "Measuring Integration Effects: A Survey," *European Economic Review*, vol. 3, November 1972, pp. 337-49; John Williamson and Anthony Bottrill, "The Impact of Customs Unions on Trade in Manufactures," *Oxford Economic Papers*, vol. 23, November 1971, pp. 323-51.

14. Manufactured products are defined as Standard International Trade Classification, Sections 5, 6, 7, and 8.

15. EFTA Secretariat, *The Effects of EFTA* (Geneva: EFTA, 1969); and *The Trade Effects of EFTA and the EEC, 1959-1967* (Geneva: EFTA, June 1972).

16. Ibid., pp. 18-19.

17. Ibid., pp. 37 and 50.

18. Our discussion is based on Edwin M. Truman, "The Production and Trade of Manufactured Products in the EEC and EFTA: A Comparison," *European Economic Review*, vol. 3, November 1972, pp. 271-90.

19. Ibid., p. 285.

20. For example, he assumes that in the absence of integration, the import shares of the various commodities would have remained the same as in 1960. Moreover, unlike the EFTA study, he does not eliminate cases of external trade creation that seem unreasonable.

21. F.J. Clavaux, "The Import Elasticity as a Yardstick for Measuring Trade Creation," *Economia Internazionale*, vol. 22, November 1969, pp. 606-12.

22. Krause, op. cit.

23. Ibid., pp. 53, 56.

24. The term "share" is a misnomer. The total food consumption is defined in the sense of the national accounts, i.e., intermediate products are not included.

25. There appears to be a shortage of good studies on trade in agricultural products. Krause (op. cit.) devotes a chapter to agriculture. His analysis is not entirely convincing for two reasons. First, he analyzes the effect of CAP on the EEC output of agricultural products. He estimates the EEC price elasticities of supply for various agricultural commodities. The elasticities are multiplied by the rate of price increase ascribed to CAP in order to determine the output effect. However, his analysis should be based on the CAP-induced rise in EEC prices relative to world prices, rather than on the absolute price increase. The available evidence suggests that, on the average, EEC producer prices did not rise more rapidly than world market prices between 1963 and 1969 (Francis Knox, *The Common Market and World Agriculture: Trade Patterns in Temperate-Zone Foodstuffs*, Praeger Special Studies in International Economics and Development [New York and London: Praeger 1972], table 17). Thus Krause's approach tends to overstate the output effects of CAP. Second, Krause determines the EEC-induced increase in the demand for agricultural products. These calculations are based on a highly questionable analysis of the income effect of integration.

26. In 1968 the EEC attempted to introduce a tax on soybeans. The plans were dropped after strong protests by the United States government.

27. On this point see Knox, op. cit., pp. 77-85.

28. For example, the German price of soft wheat was reduced by about 10 percent when CAP was introduced. See F. Baade and F. Fendt, *Die deutsche Landwirtschaft im Ringen um den Agrarmarkt Europas* (Baden-Baden: Nomos Verlag, 1971), p. 79.

29. *United States International Economic Policy in an Interdependent World*, Report to the President and Papers submitted to the Commission on International Trade and Investment Policy (Washington: U.S. Government Printing Office, July 1971).

30. OECD, op. cit.

31. Gerard Curzon, "A Zero-Tariff World," *The Journal of World Trade Law*, vol. 7, January-February 1973, pp. 1-7.

32. For an excellent analysis of the nontariff barriers to trade see Robert E. Baldwin, *Nontariff Distortions of International Trade* (Washington: The Brookings Institution, 1970).

33. OECD, op. cit., pp. 70-75.

5

The Role of the Multinational Firm in the Exports of Manufactures from Developing Countries

Benjamin I. Cohen[a]
Yale University

The Significance of U.S. Firms' Role

Despite the failure of the rich countries to give substantial general tariff preferences[1] for the exports of manufactures from less developed countries (LDCs), their exports of manufactures have grown rapidly during the last decade. While the precise rate of growth depends on one's definitions of "manufactures" and of "less developed countries," data based on General Agreement on Trade and Tariffs (GATT) definitions indicate that the value of manufactured exports by LDCs grew by about 15 percent per year during the last decade; and by 1970 manufactures accounted for about 20 percent of total LDC export earnings and about 30 percent of export earnings, excluding fuels.[2]

The LDCs have had previous spurts in their exports of specific commodities, and a large literature exists on why the rapid expansion of their exports of primary products in the nineteenth century did not lead to significant economic development in these nations. The general theme of much of this literature is that, in Kindleberger's words, "until the last few years, direct investment in the less developed countries took on an enclave character, in which foreign factors of production—management, capital, and frequently labor—were combined with limited host-country inputs such as a mineral deposit, tropical climate, or in some countries, common labor."[3]

Various writers stress different factors in explaining the development of these enclaves. Myint[4] deals with the lack of a domestic transport system and of a smoothly operating market mechanism; Myrdal notes "that the course of events took this 'colonial' character was not mainly due either to the designs of those who provided the capital and built the economic enclaves, or to the intentional policies of their governments. It was much more the natural outcome of the unhampered working of the contemporary market forces."[5] Hymer and Resnick, on the other hand, stress the deliberate policy of the governments of the colonial powers "as Europe formulated a single strategic conception for the development of the world economy and planned a new division of labor."[6] All

[a]This chapter is based on research supported by the National Science Foundation. I am solely responsible for its contents.

these writers agree that foreign firms played a significant role in the development of these enclaves.[7]

While we do not have comprehensive data on the role of multinational firms[8] in the contemporary boom in LDC exports of manufactures, there are scattered bits of evidence suggesting that these firms account for a large share of these LDC exports. Between 1965 and 1968 annual exports from developing countries by foreign affiliates of United States manufacturing firms rose from $700 million to $1.4 billion.[9] Between 1957 and 1966 Latin America's annual exports of manufactures rose from $709 million to $1,613 million, and subsidiaries of United States firms accounted for 65 percent of this increase of $804 million.[10] I estimate that in 1971 foreign firms[11] accounted for at least 15 percent of South Korea's $875 million of exports of manufactures, at least 20 percent of Taiwan's $1,428 million of exports of manufactures, and over 50 percent of Singapore's $285 million of exports of manufactures. IBM is said to have been the largest single exporter of manufactures from both Argentina and Brazil in 1969.[12] In 1969 locally-owned firms accounted for only 42 percent of $325 million of trade in manufactures within the Latin American Free Trade Association.[13]

What are the consequences for the LDCs of this role of the multinational firm? Can an "enclave" develop when the LDC exports manufactures? Consider, for example, the case of the Mexican "border" industries. Exports of manufactures to the United States under item 807.00[14] rose from $7 million in 1966 to $211 million in 1970. The Mexican value added on these exports was about one-third, almost entirely in the form of wages at rates above the Mexican average. Mexican workers in these industries spent 50 to 70 percent of their wages on United States commodities.[15] Is this a contemporary example of the nineteenth century phenomenon discussed over twenty years ago by Singer, where " ... the productive facilities for export from underdeveloped countries, which were so largely a result of foreign investment, never became a part of the internal economic structure of those underdeveloped countries themselves, except in the purely geographical and physical sense"?[16]

The next section of this chapter reviews the various theories about why firms invest overseas in order to see what consequences can be deduced from these theorems. The following section presents some empirical evidence based on my field work in South Korea, Taiwan, and Singapore and on other available empirical research. The final section is a brief conclusion on the use of incentives by LDCs to attract multinational manufacturing firms.

As indicated above, much of the exports from LDCs by multinational firms goes to other LDCs. But a large share is sold in the United States. Imports from all LDCs under tariff item 807.00 rose from $61 million in 1966 to $530 million in 1970 (though not all of these imports are from subsidiaries of United States firms). Thus future United States trade patterns are related to future LDC trade patterns.

It may be appropriate at this point to indicate why I pay little attention to the consequences of these trade and investment flows on United States workers, capitalists, consumers, etc. Partially, this omission reflects my own comparative advantage and partially it reflects a judgment that those United States citizens injured by such trade and investment could be—though may not be—assisted by the United States Government.

Models of Firm Investment

Different theoretical models lead to different deductions about the consequences of foreign corporate investment. MacDougall[17] used a one-sector model in which every firm operates in a competitive environment and maximizes profits with perfect certainty. With no change in technology and no economies of scale, additional foreign capital can then be shown to drive down the rate of profit on the initial stock of capital, raise the wage rate, and increase domestic income. As Richard Brecher pointed out, the results change as soon as one moves to a two-sector model. With linear homogeneous production functions in each sector, a "small" country (facing constant terms of trade) will find that additional foreign capital has no impact either on the distribution of income or on domestic income (since all the extra output accrues to the foreigners).

In the formal theoretical literature stemming from the Heckscher-Ohlin theory of international trade, foreign investment is seen as a substitute for foreign trade.[18,19] It follows from this vision that the opportunity to attract foreign capital, like the opportunity to engage in foreign trade, could make workers in the LDC better off by equalizing factor prices throughout the world. But just as one can specify a set of assumptions that leads to "immiserizing growth" via expanding foreign trade, so can one set up a model where foreign investment in the presence of domestic "distortions" can reduce labor's income and/or domestic income in the LDCs. The range of theoretical outcomes becomes even broader when one admits the possibility of the foreign firm's bringing a new technology as well as capital.[20]

The formal Heckscher-Ohlin theory assumes, among other things, that production functions are the same throughout the world, that every businessman maximizes profits in a world of perfect competition, and that everyone has complete knowledge of the present and future. This set of assumptions has at least two weaknesses: (1) It leads one to analyze the impact of corporate investment in terms of capital flows rather than the transfer of technology and management skills even though reported capital flows are small,[21] and (2) while it gives an insight into the consequences of attracting foreign investment by restricting imports,[22] it has difficulty in explaining why United States, European, and Japanese firms invest in LDCs in order to produce manufactures for sale in the rich countries. How are these multinational firms able to produce at lower costs than local LDC firms? Why do not importers in the rich countries buy directly from LDC firms? The answer, in my view, has two parts.

The first comes from the Hymer-Kindleberger analysis of direct foreign investment, which stresses that the foreign company has some advantage—such as better management, a better production technology, or the ownership of a brand name product—which allows it to compete with local firms even though it knows less about the LDC economy and has its headquarters thousands of miles away from the production site.[23] Thus one sees foreign investment in terms of partial monopoly rather than of perfect competition. What determines the size of the firm's monopoly profits when the initial investment is made? Will the multinational firm try to maintain its monopoly position by, for example, threatening potential LDC rivals with a price war? Kindleberger says that " . . . in the bilateral monopoly . . . game represented by direct investment in the less-developed country, there has been a steady shift in the advantages from the side of the company to that of the country."[24] His examples refer, however, to multinational firms exporting natural resources from an LDC. It is less clear that an LDC government can tax the profits of a foreign company producing manufactures for export. As *Fortune* put it, "the developing countries' contribution . . . will be reserves of low-cost and teachable labor."[25] Since there are now several LDCs[26] which have demonstrated a capacity to supply this type of labor, it is difficult for just one of them to tax the "monopoly" profits of the foreign firm.[27] The foreign firm will simply move to another LDC or arrange its "transfer prices" so as to show little profits in the LDC trying to tax the monopoly profits. Thus the direct benefits of the investment to the LDC are limited to the wages and local purchases by foreign firms; there may also be "indirect" benefits, such as the diffusion throughout the local economy of the foreign firm's technical and market knowledge, managerial skills, or trained labor force. The evidence on these points is discussed in the next section of this paper.

The second part of the answer is that multinational firms may also invest in developing countries in order to reduce the risks involved in supplying their major markets from a single source. A multinational firm may geographically diversify its production even if this diversification raises production costs above that of LDC firms. While such investments may reduce the multinational firm's global risks,[28] it may increase the LDC's risks as compared to having a local firm exporting to the rich country. The multinational firm is subject to pressures in many more countries than is the local firm, and the LDC may be viewed as marginal to the multinational firm exporting to rich countries. Stobaugh, for example, reports that one U.S. electronics firm responded to the 1969-70 decline in United States radio sales by stopping production in its new Taiwan plant rather than curtailing production in its United States plant.[29] We do not yet have any systematic comparison of the responses of local and multinational firms to shifts in world demand.

The Behavior of Local and Foreign Firms

Since alternative theoretical models lead to different consequences of foreign investment, I turn now to some preliminary results of empirical work I have done in South Korea, Taiwan, and Singapore. All three of these countries have had a rapid expansion of their manufactured exports, as shown below. In all three countries foreign firms were responsible for a significant portion of these exports in 1971: at least 15 percent in South Korea; at least 20 percent in Taiwan; and over 50 percent in Singapore. Exports by foreign firms are probably growing more rapidly than exports by local firms. For some products, such as transistors in South Korea and television sets in Taiwan, foreign firms account for over 80 percent of the value of exports, while for other commodities, such as cloth, foreign firms apparently account for a small fraction of exports.

My general approach is to compare foreign firms with local firms making the same product. The products considered are: baseball gloves, cloth, feed stuff, flour, radios, sewing machines, television sets, toys, transistors, yarn, and wigs. Thus my sample excludes petroleum and chemicals because they are not exported by local firms; all the other major commodities exported from these countries by foreign firms are included. United States firms operate in all three countries, and Japanese firms are in South Korea and Taiwan. The South Korean data are based both on factory tours and on questionnaires, and the results are reported in detail elsewhere.[30] The Singapore and Taiwan data are based on factory tours and on preliminary examination of questionnaires, and so my conclusions about these latter two countries are very tentative. The allocation of the seventy-five firms by product and nationality is shown in Table 5-2, where products are labeled to preserve confidentiality of the firms.

Table 5-1
Exports of Manufactures: South Korea, Taiwan and Singapore

	Volume (million of dollars)		Annual Percentage Change
	1967 (1)	1971 (2)	(3)
South Korea	214	875	42
Taiwan[a]	394	1,428	38
Singapore[b]	94	221	24

[a]Excluding canned pineapple, canned mushrooms, and canned bamboo shoots.
[b]Excluding rubber, petroleum, and road motor vehicles.
Sources: Bank of Korea, *Monthly Economic Statistics*, February 1972, p. 77; *Industry of Free China*, December 1972, pp. 136-137; Singapore Department of Statistics, *Monthly Digest of Statistics*, May 1972, pp. 41-42.

Table 5-2
Number of Firms Interviewed

Product	South Korea Local (1)	South Korea Foreign (2)	Taiwan Local (3)	Taiwan Foreign (4)	Singapore Local (5)	Singapore Foreign (6)	Total Local (7)	Total Foreign (8)
A	2	2	3	7	0	3	5	12
B	0	0	2	6	0	0	2	6
C	1	4	2	1	0	1	3	6
D	2	1	2	1	0	1	4	3
E	4	2	2	1	1	3	7	6
F	0	0	1	2	0	0	1	2
G	0	0	0	0	1	1	1	1
H	1	2	2	1	0	0	3	3
I	0	0	0	0	1	1	1	1
J	0	0	1	2	0	0	1	2
K	1	1	1	2	0	0	2	3
Total	11	12	16	23	3	10	30	45

By comparing foreign and local firms producing and exporting the same commodity, I assume that local firms could expand exports if there were no foreign firms. It may be objected that the local firms could not expand because of a shortage of capital. As argued above, one should look for the major contribution of foreign manufacturing firms in the areas of technology and management, not as a source of capital. The twelve foreign firms in my South Korea sample have an equity investment of only $12 million and employ 8,600 persons. I do not have similar data for my Taiwan and Singapore sample. Schreiber reports, however, that five United States firms had a total equity investment in Taiwan of $13 million, along with $7 million borrowed in the United States and $22 million borrowed in Taiwan.[31]

United States firms whose LDC foreign subsidiaries sold $276 million in manufactures to the United States in 1969 report investment in the subsidiaries of $79 million and LDC employment of 66,000.[32] We also know that United States direct investment in manufacturing in all of Asia (excluding Japan) was only $217 million during the three-year period of 1969-1971; of this amount, reinvested earnings were $119 million. A profitable local firm would presumably have reinvested also, and so the net contribution of new capital by all United States manufacturing firms in these three years was $98 million.[33] This inflow of $98 million may be compared with $62 million raised by Asian countries (excluding Japan) in the international bond market in 1969, 1970, and 1971.[34]

These countries can probably raise capital cheaper via the international bond market. The average issue yield on bonds issued by developing countries from

1969 through 1971 ranged from 6.5 percent to 8.9 percent.[35] While we do not have direct evidence on the rate of return on investments by foreign manufacturing firms in particular LDCs, the U.S. Department of Commerce estimates that between 1969 and 1971 direct investment in manufacturing in all developing countries earned 14-15 percent on the United States parent firm's investment.[36]

My tentative observations from the firms in my sample are that: (1) foreign firms tend to export a somewhat higher fraction of their output than local firms; (2) foreign firms tend to import more and to buy less from local firms than do local firms making the same product;[37] (3) local firms tend to have a higher value added per dollar of sales than foreign firms; and (4) there is no clear pattern as to whether foreign firms pay their workers more than local firms. These conclusions are subject to two caveats. The firms in my sample are all primarily exporters. The comparison between local and foreign firms may be different when they are selling mainly in local markets.[38] Most of the foreign firms are also less than five years old, and their behavior may change over time.

What about the type of technology? While foreign firms probably pay less for capital than local firms, some people argue[39] that foreign firms may know more about the worldwide stock of available techniques and be more concerned with minimizing production costs than in acquiring prestige from a "modern," capital-intensive plant. Strassman, in a study of fourteen United States firms and twenty-two Mexican firms producing in Mexico, concluded that United States firms were more likely than Mexican firms to adopt labor-intensive techniques.[40] Pack, in a study of three industries in Kenya, also found that the foreign firm was more likely to use a labor-intensive technique.[41] Wells, on the other hand, using a sample of fifty plants in six industries in Indonesia, found that foreign firms were more likely to use a capital-intensive technology.[42] Mason, in a study of fourteen United States and fourteen local firms in nine industries in Mexico and the Philippines, found that United States firms employed more building per worker and about the same amount of equipment per worker as compared to local firms.[43] Leff, in a study of twenty firms in the Brazilian capital goods industry, found that both foreign and domestic firms relied heavily on second-hand machinery imported from the rich countries.[44]

In my work I use electricity consumption per worker to measure capital-labor ratios among firms producing the same product, and I find no clear pattern. Sometimes foreign firms are more capital-intensive, sometimes local firms. These various studies seem to me to be inconclusive, perhaps because some look at firms selling only in the local market (Leff, Wells, and Pack), some look at firms concentrating on exports (Cohen), and some do not indicate the orientation of the firms in the sample (Strassman and Mason). Further empirical work is needed in this area.

What about the "indirect" or "external" consequences of direct foreign investment? Do foreign firms train local workers and/or managers who then move to local firms? Do foreign firms induce local suppliers to be more efficient? Do foreign firms demonstrate to local competitors more efficient ways of operating? My general response to this set of questions is that the answer is more likely to be affirmative when the foreign firm is the first to produce and to export the commodity.

In both Korea and Taiwan labor turnover is low. In only two Korean firms out of eighteen answering the question did more than half of the assembly line workers have previous factory experience, and both of these firms were foreign. About half the firms reported that less than 10 percent of their employees (assembly line and supervisory) had been previously employed. Only one Korean firm and one foreign firm reported that more than 10 percent of those previously employed had worked for a foreign firm. The one Korean firm was making transistors, which is the only product in my Korean sample which was initially produced in Korea by a foreign firm. Similarly in Taiwan, where television sets and transistors were the only two products first produced by foreign firms, local producers of these two commodities have many managerial and technical personnel who had previously worked for foreign firms. For the other seven commodities in my Taiwan sample which were first produced and exported by local firms, foreign firms seem more likely to take workers away from local firms than to supply them to local firms. In my Singapore sample, all products were initially produced by foreign firms.

Most assembly line workers in my sample come from rural areas in Korea and Taiwan.[45] A sample of thirty-six female workers, arbitrarily selected by me during factory tours, revealed that 52 percent of those working in Seoul had fathers who were farmers, and 85 percent of those working in other cities had fathers who were farmers. In a sample of thirty-six female workers in Taiwan, 27 percent of those working in Taipei had fathers who were farmers, as compared to 64 percent of those working in cities other than Taipei. One can only speculate as to why workers who have had no previous factory experience and frequently no previous urban experience can achieve such high levels of productivity.

In the cases of transistors in Korea, Taiwan, and Singapore and of television sets in Taiwan, foreign firms were the initial producers, and natives who worked for these foreign firms are now employed as technicians and managers by local firms. It is still too soon, however, to tell whether these local firms will be able to expand and to export in competition with the foreign firms.

A foreign sewing machine firm set up a factory in Taiwan and induced local suppliers of components to improve their quality. This improvement enabled local sewing machine firms greatly to expand their exports. This seems to be the only case where existing local firms benefitted from the arrival of a foreign competitor.

While the gross benefits to the LDC may be greater when the multinational firm invests in a product that local firms are not yet producing, the costs to the

LDC of such investment may also be higher. In the "bilateral monopoly" bargaining between the LDC government and the multinational firm, the LDC government presumably knows least about the products that have not been produced locally, and hence it is least able to evaluate the package of knowledge and management that a particular multinational firm offers. An LDC government can, for example, make a better choice among alternative foreign cotton textile firms than among alternative foreign color television firms.[46] Thus the net benefits (gross benefits minus costs) to the LDC may be no higher for foreign investment in a new product than for products already produced and exported by local firms.[47]

The LDC and the Foreign Firm

Looking at either the various theoretical models or the empirical evidence, I find it difficult to make a general comparison of the benefits to the LDC of these two alternatives: (1) having direct foreign investment for the export of manufactures; or (2) having the LDC government borrow the capital in the international bond market and the local firms either buy the technology or develop it locally. I suspect that the "narrow" economic factors discussed in the previous section explain only a small part of a LDC government's attitudes towards direct United States investment, and I have discussed elsewhere some of these other considerations for the case of South Korea.[48]

Suppose that for some set of reasons an LDC government decides it wants to attract a number of foreign firms. What policies should it adopt? South Korea, Taiwan, and Singapore all offer foreign firms five years exemption from income tax and exemption from import duties for raw materials that enter into exports.[49] Believing (or assuming?) that firms equate after-tax rates of return around the world, economic theorists tend to argue that the level of corporate income tax in a particular country will affect the inflow of foreign capital.[50] Economists who have interviewed businessmen about their investments in LDCs tend to be very skeptical that reducing the corporate income tax attracts additional foreign investment. Hughes and Seng, based on a survey of 127 firms from six countries that invested in Singapore, say " . . . foreign investors, almost without exception, stated that taxation concessions . . . did not play a significant role, and for the most part played no role at all, in bringing them to Singapore."[51] Aharoni, based on a survey of thirty-eight U.S. firms that had made over a hundred decisions about direct foreign investment, concluded " . . . that the granting of income tax exemption by foreign governments is not an important factor in foreign investment decisions."[52] Schreiber, in a study of twenty-two United States companies in Taiwan found, "while half of the reporting companies said that the tax concession was meaningful, none said that without it they would not have invested in Taiwan."[53]

Even if it were true that multinational firms respond to tax incentives in LDCs, I suggest that an LDC government need not offer tax exemption to all foreign investors. There is substantial evidence[54] that most direct foreign investment is done by firms that are in oligopolistic industries. In such industries it is quite possible that most firms will imitate the investment behavior of the firm which first invests abroad.[55] As Aharoni put it, "when several companies in the same industry went abroad, others felt compelled to follow suit in order to maintain their relative size and their relative rate of growth. . . . Imitating the commitments of a leader on the grounds that one is less vulnerable if his exposures are the same as those of his principal competitors."[56] Those readers who find this point obvious may skip the next two paragraphs.

One can make more formal the notion that in an uncertain world firms in an oligopolistic industry will follow any firm which invests abroad. Consider an industry with two United States firms, each of which sells in the United States and is deciding whether to continue production in the United States or to invest in a LDC for export to the United States. Suppose total industry sales are independent of production costs (at least within the range considered in this example). Each firm faces two kinds of uncertainty: what will its rival do and how will costs in the LDC compare with those in the United States. The latter uncertainty stems from such factors as the future of the exchange rate for the dollar, future United States tariff levels, and future productivity levels and wages in the LDC relative to those in the United States. Each firm is assumed to perceive the same "payoff" matrix, as shown below:

Table 5-3
Payoff Matrix

			Firm B's Profits			
			Invest in LDC		Do not Invest in LDC	
			LDC is low cost	LDC is high cost	LDC is low cost	LDC is high cost
Firm A's profits	invest in LDC	LDC is low cost	12, 12	–	20, 4	–
		LDC is high cost	–	5, 5	–	4, 20
	do not invest in LDC	LDC is low cost	4, 20	–	10, 10	–
		LDC is high cost	–	20, 4	–	10, 10

Firm A's profits are shown to the left, and firm B's profits to the right. For example, if firm A invests in the LDC and firm B does not, and if costs in the LDC turn out to be lower than costs in the United States, then firm A's profits are $20 and firm B has profits of $4. If firm A invests in the LDC and firm B does not, and if production costs in the LDC turn out to be higher than in the United States, then firm A earns $4 and firm B earns $20.

Suppose each firm follows a strategy of maximizing its minimum profit. If firm B thinks firm A will invest in the LDC, then firm B will also invest, since investing implies a profit for firm B of at least $5, as compared to a possible profit of only $4 if it does not invest. If firm B thinks firm A will not invest in the LDC, then firm B will also not invest in the LDC. Therefore, once firm A invests, firm B will also invest, even though firm B is still uncertain as to whether production costs will be lower in the LDC than in the United States. Similarly, if firm B invests first in the LDC, firm A will follow suit.

It follows from this type of analysis that the LDC governments need only offer tax concessions to the first foreign investor in the industry. Since in reality most industries have more than two firms, it might be necessary to offer incentives to the first, say, three foreign firms. Such a policy might even accelerate the decision to invest in the LDCs, since each foreign firm would strive to be one of the first three to invest. This type of analysis could also be extended to other "concessions" granted to foreign firms by a LDC government, such as permission for the foreign firm to have 100 percent of the equity in the LDC company. However, as noted above, a single LDC cannot act alone in taxing foreign firms which are exporting manufactures. One can only speculate on whether the LDC governments will be able to form a common policy towards multinational manufacturing firms and thereby increase the benefits they receive from investments by these firms.

Notes

1. The preference scheme introduced by the European Economic Community in 1971 will not, under its present arrangements, have much impact on LDC exports. See Richard N. Cooper, "The European Community's System of Generalized Tariff Preferences: A Critique," (New Haven: Yale Economic Growth Center Discussion Paper no. 132, November 1971).

2. Exports of manufactures (iron and steel, chemicals, engineering products, road motor vehicles, textiles and clothing, and other manufactures) by LDCs rose from $3.5 billion in 1963 to $9.8 billion in 1970. Their exports of fuels were $18 billion in 1970, and their total exports were $55 billion in 1970. Data from *International Trade 1970* (Geneva: GATT, 1971), p. 23 and *International Trade 1971* (Geneva: GATT, 1972), p. 15.

3. Charles P. Kindleberger, *American Business Abroad* (New Haven: Yale University Press, 1969), p. 146.

4. Hla Myint, "The 'Classicial Theory' of International Trade and the Underdeveloped Countries," *Economic Journal*, vol. 78, June 1968, reprinted in Richard E. Caves and Harry G. Johnson, eds., *Readings in International Economics* (Homewood, Illinois: Irwin, 1968), pp. 318-338.

5. Gunnar Myrdal, *An International Economy, Problems and Prospects* (New York: Harper and Brothers, 1956), p. 100.

6. Stephen Hymer and Stephen Resnick, "International Trade and Uneven Development," in Jagdish Bhagwati, ed., et al., *Trade, Balance of Payments, and Growth* (Amsterdam: North Holland, 1971), p. 483.

7. As the cases of Argentina, Australia, and Canada indicate, an export boom under the auspices of Europeans can facilitate economic development when the original native population is negligible.

8. Unless otherwise stated, in this chapter a multinational firm is one that has production facilities in at least two countries.

9. *Survey of Current Business*, vol. 50, October 1970, p. 20.

10. *The Effects of United States and Other Foreign Investments in Latin America* (New York: The Council for Latin America, Inc., 1970), p. 29.

11. Unless otherwise stated, in this paper a foreign firm is a firm not wholly owned by local citizens. Anecdotal evidence indicates that some firms considered local by LDC governments are in fact controlled by foreigners; this may be especially important in textiles because of the way LDC governments allocate their export quotas under the International Textile Agreement.

12. Testimony of John Tuthill in U.S. Congress, Joint Economic Committee, *U.S. Policies Towards Developing Countries* (Washington: U.S. Government Printing Office, May 1970), p. 729.

13. Juan Carlos Casas, "Las Multinacionales y el Comercio Latinoamericano." *Cemla Boletin Mensual*, vol. 18, December 1972, pp. 605-614. I owe this reference to Carlos Diaz-Alejandro.

14. Item 807.00 concerns the United States tariff on the foreign value added of United States imports of items fabricated from United States components.

15. Data for 1966 United States imports and for the import component of Mexican wages from U.S. Tariff Commission, *Economic Factors Affecting the Use of 807.00 and 806.30* (Washington: U.S. Tariff Commission, September 1970), pp. 66, 180. I owe this reference to Kenneth Jameson. Data for 1970 United States imports kindly supplied by U.S. Tariff Commission.

16. H.W. Singer, "The Distribution of Gains Between Investing and Borrowing Countries," *American Economic Review*, vol. 40, May 1950, reprinted in Caves and Johnson, op. cit., p. 308.

17. G.D.A. MacDougall, "The Benefits and Costs of Private Investment from Abroad: A Theoretical Approach," *Economic Record*, vol. 36, March 1960, reprinted in Caves and Johnson, op. cit., pp. 172-194.

18. See, for example, Robert Mundell, "International Trade and Factor Mobility," *American Economic Review*, vol. 47, June 1957, reprinted in Caves and Johnson, op. cit., pp. 101-114.

19. Ohlin, tempering formal logic with empirical observation, was more cautious. Observing that there were many factors at work, he concluded that "the tendency toward a reduction of trade may be counteracted by a tendency to increased trade. . . ." Bertil Ohlin, *Interregional and International Trade*, rev. ed. (Cambridge: Harvard University Press, 1967), p. 215.

20. Benjamin I. Cohen, "An Alternative Theoretical Approach to the Impact of Foreign Investment on the Host Country," (New Haven: Yale Economic Growth Center Discussion Paper no. 164, November 1972).

21. In 1971 United States direct investment in manufacturing in all developing countries was $521 million, of which 53 percent represented retained earnings; United States firms also borrow locally to finance investments in LDCs. For example, in 1970 United States manufacturing affiliates in Latin America spent $669 million on plant and equipment; net capital outflows from the United States were $100 million; retained earnings were $200 million, and the balance was financed by borrowing outside the United States and by depreciation allowances. Data from *Survey of Current Business*, vol. 52, November 1972, and *Survey of Current Business*, vol. 52, March 1972.

22. See Mundell, op. cit., pp. 111-114.

23. For an exposition of this theory, see Charles P. Kindleberger, *American Business Abroad* (New Haven: Yale University Press, 1969), pp. 11-33.

24. Ibid., p. 150.

25. "The Poor Countries Turn from Buy-Less to Sell-More," *Fortune*, vol. 81, April 1970, p. 91.

26. Such as South Korea, Taiwan, Singapore, Mexico, and Brazil.

27. This statement is true only for those United States firms which do not immediately repatriate their LDC profits to the United States. For those United States firms which do immediately repatriate these profits, the method of calculating the credit against the United States corporate tax for income taxes paid to LDC governments permits the United States firm to minimize its total tax payments only if it pays some income tax to the LDC. See the discussion in Robert Hellawell, "United States Income Taxation and Less Developed Countries: A Critical Appraisal," *Columbia Law Review*, vol. 66, December 1966, esp. pp. 1395-1398.

28. For evidence on this point, see Benjamin I. Cohen, "Foreign Investments by United States Corporations as a Way of Reducing Risk," (New Haven: Yale Economic Growth Center Discussion Paper no. 151, September 1972).

29. Robert B. Stobaugh, "How Investment Abroad Creates Jobs at Home," *Harvard Business Review*, vol. 50, September-October 1972, pp. 122-123.

30. Benjamin I. Cohen, "Comparative Behavior of Foreign and Domestic Export Firms in a Developing Economy," *Review of Economics and Statistics*, vol. 55, May 1973.

31. Jordan Schreiber, *U.S. Corporate Investment in Taiwan* (Cambridge: Harvard University Press, 1970), p. 51.

32. U.S. Tariff Commission, op. cit., pp. 152, 164.

33. The picture is similar in Latin America. Direct investment in manufacturing by United States firms was $1,102 million in 1969-1971, of which $685 million was reinvested earnings. Data from *Survey of Current Business*, vol. 52, November 1972, pp. 29, 31 and *Survey of Current Business*, vol. 51, October 1971, p. 35.

34. Latin American countries raised $469 million in the international bond market in 1969, 1970, and 1971, as compared to $417 million of new foreign capital via United States manufacturing corporations in the same three years. International Bank for Reconstruction and Development, *Annual Report of the World Bank*, 1972 (Washington: IBRD, 1972), p. 93.

35. Ibid., p. 94.

36. Earnings are broadly defined and include branch earnings, dividends paid by the foreign subsidiary to the parent, reinvested earnings by the subsidiary, interest paid by the subsidiary to the parent, and royalties and fees paid by the subsidiary to the parent. *Survey of Current Business*, vol. 52, November 1972, p. 23.

37. This second finding is also true in Canada. *A Citizen's Guide to the Gray Report* (Toronto: The Canadian Forum, 1970), p. 59.

38. Katz, for example, finds that in the Argentina pharmaceutical industry foreign firms pay higher wages. J. Katz, *Importacion de Tecnologie, Aprendizaje local e Industrializacion dependiente* (Buenos Aires: Instituto DiTella, 1972).

39. Ian Little, Tibor Scitovsky, and Maurice Scott, *Industry and Trade In Some Developing Counties: A Comparative Study* (London: Oxford University Press, 1970), p. 57.

40. W. Paul Strassman, *Technological Change and Economic Development* (Ithaca, New York: Cornell University Press, 1968), pp. 190-194.

41. Howard Pack, "Employment in Kenyan Manufacturing—Some Microeconomic Evidence," (mimeo, April 1972).

42. Though he explains this result in terms of foreign firms being more likely to have "monopoly" profits because they make consumer products with an internationally known brand name. Louis T. Wells, Jr., "Economic Man and Engineering Man: Choice of Technology in a Low Wage Country," (mimeo, November 1972).

43. R. Hal Mason, "The Transfer of Technology through Direct Foreign Investment and the Factor Proportions Problem in Developing Countries," (mimeo, October 1970), pp. 53-63.

44. Nathaniel Leff, *The Brazilian Capital Goods Industry, 1929-1964* (Cambridge: Harvard University Press, 1968), p. 27.

45. Singapore, a city-state of 2.1 million persons, has no significant rural population.

46. Individuals face the same problem. For most purchases the consumer can easily learn about the relative quality of similar products and compare the quality with the price. For those products a competitive private marketplace gives an "efficient" result. As Arrow noted, for some consumer purchases, such as medical care, the private marketplace is less likely to give an "efficient" result because "the value of information is frequently not known in any meaningful sense to the buyer; if, indeed, he knew enough to measure the value of information, he would know the information itself." Kenneth J. Arrow, "Uncertainty and the Welfare Economics of Medical Care," *American Economic Review*, vol. 53, December 1963, p. 946.

47. This type of analysis suggests that a LDC, because it knows less about the technology than a rich country, will pay a multinational firm more than will a rich country. Johnson, using a different framework, reaches the opposite conclusion: that the LDC will pay less than the rich country for a particular "package" of knowledge and skill. Harry G. Johnson, "The Efficiency and Welfare Implications of the Multinational Firms," in Charles P. Kindleberger *The International Corporation*, ed. (Cambridge: M.I.T. Press, 1970), p. 41.

48. Benjamin I. Cohen, "Comparative Behavior of Foreign and Domestic Export Firms in a Developing Economy," *Review of Economics and Statistics*, vol. 55, May 1973, p. 196.

49. These three governments also allow foreign firms to have 100 percent of the equity in the investment.

50. Theorists sometimes note that a double taxation agreement or a tax credit scheme by the parent country's government will make the geographic allocation of investment independent of the LDC's tax rate (if the LDC tax rate is below that of the parent country). See for example, MacDougall, op. cit., pp. 175-176. As noted earlier, this argument implicitly assumes that the multinational firm immediately repatriates the profits it earns in the LDC.

51. Helen Hughes and You Poh Seng, eds., *Foreign Investment and Industrialisation in Singapore* (Canberra: Australian National University Press, 1969), p. 183.

52. Yair Aharoni, *The Foreign Investment Decision Process* (Cambridge, Mass.: Harvard University Graduate School of Business Administration, 1966), p. 235.

53. Jordan Schreiber, *U.S. Corporate Investment in Taiwan* (Cambridge, Mass.: Harvard University Press, 1970), p. 75.

54. See, for example, Raymond Vernon, *Sovereignty at Bay* (New York: Basic Books, 1971), esp. Chs. 1 and 3.

55. Fifteen years ago Duesenberry argued that in an oligopolistic industry "it is important . . . for every firm to cut costs as fast as its rivals do. But that can be achieved equally well whether all the firms follow cautious policy and reduce costs slowly, or adopt a daring policy and reduce costs rapidly . . . the firm which is willing to take the greatest risks will set the pace of investment and

research expenditures which in the long run set the level of costs." James Duesenberry, *Business Cycles and Economic Growth* (New York: McGraw-Hill, 1958), pp. 130-131.

56. Aharoni, op. cit., pp. 65-66.

U.S. Trade with Latin America and the New Role of the Multinational Enterprise

Kenneth Johnson
University of Notre Dame

Introduction

Their geographic proximity and basically complementary economies have resulted in a close economic relationship between the Latin American economies and the United States. With some few exceptions, e.g. Argentina during the second World War, the United States has been the dominant external economic force in the various Latin Republics. As a group the Latin American countries have also been among the most important partners for the United States. There have long been significant United States investments in Latin America, and prior to World War II Latin America was the area of greatest investment by United States firms. Similarly, the share of Latin America in United States trade has been substantial, generally constituting over 25 percent of total United States imports and exports.[1] For specific commodities, some of which are now categorized as "strategic commodities," the importance of Latin America has been even greater.

This historically close relationship takes on a new importance in light of the current adjustments being carried out in the area of international economic relations. In the effort to attain a new equilibrium in trade and payments, the relationships of the United States with each of its main trading areas becomes a matter of direct concern. While total balance in payments can be effected by exchange rate adjustment, trade with given areas will be affected differentially, depending on the types of goods traded, the general trends in that trade, and the actions of the various trading partners.[2] Thus in this chapter the underlying relationships in U.S.-L.A. trade will be examined in order better to understand the likely outlines of trade as the new equilibrium is approached. Also, a new factor in this trade will be examined in two of the more important trading partners, Brazil and Mexico. This is the multinational enterprise with its role in the exports of Latin American countries. It will be demonstrated that these descendents of United States foreign investment are playing a new and potentially quite significant role in exports from certain Latin American countries, particularly in exports of manufactured products.

The chapter will first examine the general trends in trade between the United

61

States and Latin America and will then focus on the individual Latin American countries and individual commodity groups. Last to be examined is the operation of multinational enterprises in Brazil and Mexico.

General Outlines of Trading Relations

In view of the difficulties of the United States with her balance of trade, one aspect of trade relations with Latin America is particularly important, i.e., in ten of the twelve years from 1960 to 1971 the United States was in surplus on her trade in goods and services with Latin America. More importantly, the general trend of the surplus (see Table 6-1) was toward greater surplus, rising from a negative $50 million in 1960 to a positive $868 million in 1970. In some years the surplus with Latin America was almost as great as the entire United States surplus in trade, and the $756 million surplus in 1971 was in direct contrast to a hefty 1971 United States deficit in trade.

Table 6-1
Latin American Trade with the United States (all in millions of dollars)

Year	I Imports into U.S.	II Exports to L.A.	III Net Trade with Latin America	IV Total U.S. Trade Surplus
1960	3600	3550	−50	4906
1961	3270	3490	220	5588
1962	3300	3280	−20	4561
1963	3380	3240	120	5241
1964	3400	3770	370	6831
1965	3530	3730	200	4942
1966	3890	4170	180	3824
1967	3770	4080	310	3817
1968	4060	4660	600	612
1969	4214	4807	593	621
1970	4779	5647	868	2164
1971	4881	5617	736	−2105

Source:
Columns I-III
United Nations Commission on Trade and Development, *Handbook of International Trade and Development Statistics, 1969* (New York: United Nations, 1969) and U.S. Department of Commerce, *US Exports:-World Area by Schedule by Grouping* (Washington: U.S. Government Printing Office, 1961-72), and U.S. Department of Commerce, *US General Imports: World Area by Commodity Grouping* (Washington: U.S. Government Printing Office, 1961-72).
Column IV
U.S. Council of Economic Advisors, *Economic Report of the President, 1973* (Washington: U.S. Government Printing Office, 1973).

Barring cataclysmic changes in trading relations, it is unlikely that the United States will move from a surplus to a deficit in her trade with Latin America. Significant changes in the opposite direction are equally unlikely, as witness the care with which Latin countries have maintained par between their currencies and the dollar during the recent monetary adjustments.

More important for our purposes, however, is an evaluation of the shares of the United States and of Latin America in each other's trade. It is here that major changes are occurring and here that the trade prospects for the 1970s will be defined.

The figures in Table 6-2 show that during the 1960s imports from Latin America averaged 18.4 percent of total imports into the United States, while Latin America took 14.6 percent of all United States exports. However, the United States provided 40.5 percent of Latin American imported goods and took 34.7 percent of Latin America's exports. Thus the United States' share of the Latin American market is much greater than their share of the United States market.[3,4]

Examination of the time trends of these shares shows that from the perspective of both the United States and of Latin America, their bilateral trade is decreasing in relative importance. Over the decade, Latin America's share of

Table 6-2
Relative Importance of U.S. and L.A. in Each Other's Trade

	I Imports from L.A. as % of Total Imports into U.S.	II Exports to L.A. as % of Total U.S. Exports	III Imports from U.S. as % of Total L.A. Imports	IV Exports to U.S. as % of Total L.A. Exports
1960	.242	.173	.447	.419
1961	.224	.167	.417	.375
1962	.207	.152	.399	.359
1963	.203	.140	.399	.347
1964	.186	.143	.412	.320
1965	.168	.137	.400	.319
1966	.157	.139	.400	.333
1967	.144	.130	.385	.321
1968	.126	.136	.388	.334
1969	.116	.128	.424	.334
1970	.119	.132	.432	.348
1971	.107	.129	.388	.346

Source: United Nations Commission on Trade and Development, *Handbook of International Trade and Development Statistics, 1969* (New York: United Nations, 1969) and U.S. Department of Commerce, *US Exports:-World Area by Schedule by Grouping* (Washington: U.S. Government Printing Office, 1961-72) and U.S. Department of Commerce, *US General Imports: World Area by Commodity Grouping* (Washington: U.S. Government Printing Office, 1961-72).

United States imports fell from 24 percent to 11 percent. This was the most significant decline, but the other shares decreased as well. Latin America's share of United States exports fell from 17 percent to 13 percent, while the United States in 1970 took 35 percent as opposed to 42 percent of Latin American exports. Similarly, the United States supplied 39 percent of Latin American imports in 1970, down from 45 percent in 1960.

An examination of the major trends in world trade provides a ready explanation of these tendencies. The outstanding characteristic of trade during the 1960s was the very rapid increase in trade in manufactured products. Since this is a type of good which has not generally been exported from Latin America, the decline in Latin America's role in United States imports would be expected.[5] Couple this with the rapid growth in income in Europe and Japan and their increasing ability to compete with the United States, and the overall decrease in the importance of their trade is not surprising.

However, such trends raise the question as to whether the United States trade relationship with Latin America is dwindling into insignificance. While no definitive answer to this question can be offered, it seems unlikely that the respective roles of the two partners will continue to decrease. Indeed all the evidence which will be presented in this paper on the policies being undertaken by the countries involved, the underlying patterns in the commercial shifts within Latin America, and the types of growth in Latin American trade indicate that there should be little additional erosion of the importance of this portion of United States trade, and that trade with Latin America may indeed increase in importance.[6]

Trade by Country and by Trading Partner

A view of the experience of the individual Latin countries during the 1960s gives an indication of how the relationship between that area and the United States is changing and allows some insights into the implications of this change for the future. The broad results can be summarized as follows:

1. There has been steady growth in Latin American exports and imports, but trade with the United States has in general failed to grow as rapidly as average trade.

2. A major factor in this development has been the Central American Common Market, which accounted for significant portions of the increase in trade in the area of most rapid growth, Central America.

3. In other countries there has been a shift toward other trading partners such as Japan and the Eastern bloc, though major diversion has not occurred.

4. The evidence available at this point indicates that the decline in mutual shares should stop or even reverse itself in the 1970s.

Examination of the trade data will exhibit the above tendencies. From Table

6-3 it can be seen that the growth in the value of exports from the Latin American countries between 1960 and 1969 averaged 5.5 percent per year. In volume terms the increase was 4.8 percent per year, the difference reflecting an improvement in the Latin American terms of trade. Both of these rates of increase were higher than the corresponding increases during the previous decade, which were 3.7 percent and 4.1 percent respectively. The median increase in value over the period was 8 percent per year. At the high end of the scale we find Bolivia with a 13.6 percent rise, Panama 13.2 percent, and Honduras 11.2 percent. At the low end are Haiti, a 1.3 percent decline, and Venezuela, a .5 percent rise. There is a significant price effect in these figures, however. In volume terms all of the Central American countries had relatively high rates of growth, the lowest being El Salvador, whose 7.8 percent is higher than the highest South American country. Thus, the Central American export performance is quite significant. In the cases of Bolivia, Chile, and Peru, the growth is very significantly greater in value terms than in volume terms, reflecting the influence of the Vietnam war on their mineral exports.

Turning to the import performance, it is seen that the imports in value terms increased at a 5.5 percent rate and the volume at a 4.2 percent annual rate. The basic similarity of the basket of imports precluded the wide variance over countries between value and volume seen in the export figures, though the Central American countries had a more rapid rise in their imports. Generally there was a close relation between imports and exports, though Ecuador and Dominican Republic had more rapid rises in imports than exports and Chile and Brazil exhibited export growth greater than import growth.

Thus the general experience of the 1960s was one of relatively steady growth in exports and imports, with the Central American countries showing the greatest buoyancy. In some countries improvements in the price of exports played a major role in this pattern, but in virtually every country there was an increase and at a rate more rapid than during the previous decade.

Turning to the trade with the United States, Table 6-3 indicates that in general the rate of increase of this trade was slower than the overall increase. This accounts for the declining weight of trade between the two areas noted in an earlier section. There are a few exceptions to this trend. On the import side, Argentina and Uruguay had a more rapid increase in imports from the United States. On the export side, Venezuela, Peru, Bolivia, Uruguay and Paraguay and the Dominican Republic saw a more than proportional increase in their exports to the United States. Hence in certain cases particular factors offset the general pattern.

Nonetheless it is worthwhile to indicate the trading partners which accorded most of the growth in Latin American trade. (See Table 6-4.) The most dramatic changes have been in the countries of the Central American Common Market. The share of their trade with Latin America (primarily the other members of the Common Market) increased significantly in every case, the export share more

Table 6-3
Latin America: Growth of the External Sector, 1960-69 (Annual Percentages)

	Exports of Goods and Services		Indexes for the Terms of Trade 1955-59 = 100		Imports of Goods and Services		Value of Growth in Trade with U.S., 1958-68 (Annual Percentages)	
	Current Value 1960-69	Volume 1960-69	1960-65	1965-69	Current Value 1960-69	Volume 1960-69	Exports	Imports
Argentina	4.4	3.7	116	116	3.4	3.1	3.17%	3.30%
Bolivia	13.6	6.7	113	160	10.3	9.2	24.37	5.23
Brazil	6.4	6.4	84	79	3.7	2.7	1.74	4.18
Colombia	4.2	4.7	83	78	4.5	3.6	-2.66	3.61
Costa Rica	9.3	9.3	77	75	9.6	8.9	7.60	5.88
Chile	9.7	4.5	99	136	5.8	5.2	3.43	3.38
Ecuador	3.0	3.1	84	80	7.1	6.8	.88	7.54
El Salvador	7.5	7.8	78	78	6.4	5.2	-1.08	1.69
Guatemala	9.7	10.9	68	63	8.1	6.9	-1.01	1.46
Haiti	-1.3	-1.6	81	77	0.5	-0.5	1.57	0.00
Honduras	11.3	8.7	88	94	11.4	10.8	8.37	7.50
Mexico	8.0	5.6	92	89	7.5	4.0	4.67	4.22
Nicaragua	10.2	9.1	93	97	10.0	9.9	10.00	6.29
Panama	13.2	11.3	87	91	10.7	9.5	15.86	8.57
Paraguay	6.7	5.3	76	77	6.9	6.1	5.00	6.36
Peru	8.6	4.0	94	123	8.3	7.8	20.81	1.76
Dominican Republic	3.2	-0.3	98	111	10.7	12.0	10.13	4.06
Uruguay	4.8	4.3	114	108	0.0	-0.7	10.13	4.06
Venezuela	0.5	2.8	75	56	4.2	1.7	.05	-.38
Latin America excluding Cuba	5.5	4.8	86.6	85.1	5.5	4.2	2.60	2.91

Source: United Nations Economic Commission for Latin America, *Economic Survey of Latin America, 1970* (New York: United Nations, 1972), p. 74.

than tripling in all cases, and the share of imports increasing apace with the exception of Honduras. Thus the decline in the United States share of trade with these countries is a direct result of the mercuric growth of intramarket trade.[7]

In the case of the rest of Latin America, such easily isolated effects are not apparent. The shift in these cases seems due to the entry into trade of several new partners, Japan and Eastern Europe, as well as the growth in trade between the LAFTA countries. Looking at the data, one sees that in all cases there have been increases in the share of the Japanese and the Eastern European countries. In most cases the sum of the trade with these two still is less than 10 percent, with Ecuador's 23.2 percent and Peru's 17.2 percent being the notable exceptions in terms of Latin exports. However, as noted above, the entry of these areas into trade in manufactures and the import of required raw materials makes this growth understandable.

With regard to the Latin American Free Trade Association, on the export side Mexico, Colombia, and Argentina exhibit major increases in the LAFTA share, doubling or—in Colombia's case—increasing fivefold. On the import side Mexico, Venezuela, Chile, Peru, and Ecuador saw major increases in the share coming from the rest of Latin America. However, in many cases the shares of trade of LAFTA countries with Latin America actually fell quite significantly. Peru, Bolivia, and Paraguay all had significant drops in export shares. Brazil, Bolivia, and Uruguay all had major declines in import shares. Thus the significant impact on trading shares seen in the Central American Common Market was not present in the case of the LAFTA countries. The explanation for the declining importance of the United States in overall trade is the growth of the role of Japan and Eastern Europe and some reorientation within LAFTA. The remaining shift has come in the trade with Europe; but this has again varied across countries, and in combination with the shifts in LAFTA trade it has not offset the decline in the share of the United States in Latin American trade.

The implications of these developments for trade with the United States present some difficulty. The currency realignments will certainly act against increases in Japanese and European trade; however, basic economic factors would still seem likely to lead to rapid trade increases. In the case of LAFTA, it is apparent by now that few additional increases in trade can be expected except within the Andean Group, which must as yet be considered an unproven attempt at regional integration. However, it is unlikely that an upsurge similar to that in Central America will occur in this area.

Several other factors add to the impression that there will be little additional erosion in the trading relationships of the United States and Latin America. For example, in 1973, for the first time since trade preferences for manufactures became a major concern of developing countries, the United States government announced that such preferences for Latin America were acceptable to the United States. Thus it is likely that such goods from Latin America will receive preferences during the 1970s, a policy which will increase the Latin American

Table 6-4

Latin America: Destination of Exports and Origin of Imports, by Principal Regions and Countries, 1958 and 1968 (Percentage Shares)

| | United States | | | | EEC+EFTA | | | |
| | 1958 | | 1968 | | 1958 | | 1968 | |
	Exports	Imports	Exports	Imports	Exports	Imports	Exports	Imports
Total Latin America	45.6	50.2	35.5	38.5	26.4	27.4	28.6	27.3
LAFTA countries	42.6	49.6	36.6	42.5	27.6	30.1	31.1	30.3
Mexico	76.2	77.0	65.6	63.1	10.9	16.9	15.2	25.0
Colombia	69.2	59.5	41.9	50.4	19.3	29.5	34.2	23.6
Ecuador	58.5	51.0	40.8	38.1	29.2	36.5	23.2	34.9
Brazil	43.0	35.7	33.3	32.1	29.8	27.9	36.1	32.2
Venezuela	42.1	57.3	42.9	50.5	14.5	33.1	16.4	32.1
Peru	38.1	47.3	39.5	33.8	36.0	35.4	30.7	31.1
Argentina	12.4	16.5	11.8	23.1	60.2	40.4	46.5	36.7
Bolivia	32.0	52.5	35.3	42.1	54.0	22.6	50.3	27.6
Uruguay	7.9	10.5	12.3	22.4	49.0	28.9	51.9	29.1
Chile	40.4	51.6	22.4	38.4	45.0	27.6	51.4	28.1
Paraguay	23.5	28.2	25.0	24.7	26.5	20.5	29.1	30.1
CACM countries	50.8	55.8	32.8	38.3	31.8	23.0	21.9	19.4
Guatemala	64.5	59.7	27.9	41.1	27.1	24.9	19.9	24.6
Honduras	62.3	64.0	43.9	45.4	11.6	6.7	28.4	12.4
Costa Rica	50.0	51.5	47.1	38.2	35.9	28.3	16.3	19.8
El Salvador	39.7	49.1	19.4	29.2	39.6	29.6	23.2	20.7
Nicaragua	36.5	55.1	29.3	37.8	41.2	19.2	22.3	17.3
Panama	90.6	54.4	79.8	39.0				
Cuba	66.8	69.8	—	—	11.9	11.7	8.4	14.3
Dominican Republic	52.9	61.4	89.0	55.3	34.5	20.8	4.9	20.6
Haiti	48.7	62.8	61.1	61.4	46.8	16.3	26.8	20.5

| Eastern Europe | | | | Japan | | | | Latin America | | | |
| 1958 | | 1968 | | 1958 | | 1968 | | 1958 | | 1968 | |
Exports	Imports	Exports	Imports	Exports	Imports	Exports	Imports	Exports	Imports	Exports	Imports
1.9	1.2	6.2	8.6	2.0	1.6	5.2	4.2	9.1	–	11.6	–
2.0	1.5	2.5	1.6	1.3	1.6	5.0	4.2	10.3	–	11.0	–
0.1	0.2	0.2	0.3	3.7	0.7	5.7	3.9	4.5	0.9	9.1	2.6
0.4	0.5	3.8	2.6	0.2	1.0	1.6	3.4	1.5	4.5	7.9	4.0
–	–	11.8	1.2	0.7	1.0	11.4	6.6	9.6	2.9	8.5	11.0
3.7	2.1	6.5	4.4	2.0	2.4	3.1	3.4	11.7	18.3	-10.4	13.7
–	0.1	–	0.5	–	1.7	1.9	6.0	10.8	1.4	7.7	2.9
–	0.3	2.4	1.0	2.7	1.8	14.8	6.3	14.8	7.6	6.0	17.3
6.4	4.5	3.7	1.2	2.5	1.5	2.1	3.6	13.3	23.1	24.9	23.8
–	–	–	1.3	–	2.5	3.2	11.2	12.0	18.8	8.3	12.5
20.9	5.3	3.9	1.2	0.5	–	1.1	0.6	10.1	40.8	11.2	26.7
–	0.5	0.1	0.4	–	2.9	13.3	1.7	9.8	13.3	10.0	25.6
–	–	–	–	–	–	–	–	41.2	23.1	31.2	21.9
–	–	1.8	0.1	5.6	3.5	9.4	7.4	7.2	–	28.6	–
–	–	1.4	–	2.8	0.7	10.8	8.9	4.7	6.0	32.9	20.6
–	–	–	0.5	2.9	5.3	3.9	5.4	14.5	9.3	23.3	29.7
–	–	1.2	–	–	5.1	1.2	7.1	6.5	6.1	24.4	31.1
–	–	5.7	–	11.2	4.6	7.1	7.5	6.9	13.9	40.8	39.2
–	–	–	–	11.1	3.8	26.1	7.6	4.8	10.3	16.6	34.1
–	–	–	–	–	2.9	–	4.5	3.1	2.9	3.2	25.5
2.5	0.2	73.2	79.8	6.4	–	3.8	0.3	1.3	10.2	–	0.2
–	0.7	–	–	4.4	2.9	0.6	5.9	0.7	2.9	–	5.6
–	–	–	–	–	–	5.6	6.8	–	–	–	–

Source: United Nations, Economic Commission for Latin America, *Economic Survey of Latin America, 1970* New York: United Nations, 1972), pp. 92-93.

share of this important trade category. Also, the growth of the United States multinational in these countries will serve to increase the mutual relations between the United States and these countries, as will be shown in later sections.

In summation, there has been a rather significant decline in the importance of the United States and Latin America in each other's trade, a trend seen most clearly in the Central American area. However, for the 1970s, the evidence indicates that this trend will slow or even reverse itself.

Manufactured Exports From Latin America

Another important dimension of trade with Latin America is its commodity composition, particularly of trade with the United States. There has been a great desire in Latin America and other LDCs to increase their exports of manufactured products, a desire expressed most clearly at the three meetings of the United Nations Commission on Trade and Development (UNCTAD). The origin of this consideration is the awareness in these countries of the buoyancy of trade in manufactures during the 1960s (the share of manufactures in total world trade rose from 50 percent in 1955 to 70 percent in 1970), as well as a feeling that diversification away from simple unprocessed goods is a necessity for the development of a modern economy.

The general findings obtained from a breakdown of Latin trade by commodity classification are:

1. There has been growth in manufactured exports in almost every country of Latin America, and at a rate that is greater than its historical rate and greater than the rate for all trade. Thus the share of manufactures did increase during the 1960s.

2. The primary area of growth of manufactured exports has been in intra-Latin American trade. This may be an indication that the manufactured exports are not being produced so as to be competitive on the international market, but are taking advantage of trade controls to assure their market. Thus it is questionable if the above trends indicate growth in a pattern desired by the Latin American countries, growth that will lead to increasing manufactured exports to the developed countries.

For our purposes, manufactured exports are those in SITC categories 5, 6, 7, and 8, with the exception of 68. Table 6-5 indicates that there was growth in exports in these categories. During the 1960s, such trade increased by as much as 9.2 percent per year in certain countries, and in some individual countries certain categories such as chemicals (SITC 5) and machinery (SITC 7) increased by over 10 percent. The total Latin rate of increase was 4.7 percent per year; in chemicals it was 8.2 percent and in machinery 4.4 percent.[8] By historical standards this growth is respectable for Latin America, though it is still slower than that of the rest of the world. At any rate, it is far below what Latin

Table 6-5
Latin American Exports of Manufactured Goods

Country	Exports (millions of dollars)		As % of Total Exports	
	1960	1969	1960	1969
Argentina	42.9	195.6	3.9	12.1
Bolivia	–	2.8	–	1.9
Brazil	25.8	225.5	3.6	9.7
Colombia	6.9	53.3	1.4	9.5
Chile	–	41.1	–	3.8
Ecuador	2.1	2.6	1.4	1.4
Paraguay	–	4.0	–	8.4
Peru	–	6.0	–	0.7
Uruguay	–	20.4	–	11.4
Venezuela	–	32.4	–	1.1
Costa Rica	0.2	32.1	1.1	16.9
El Salvador	6.4	63.0	5.5	31.1
Guatemala	2.2	51.3	1.9	22.0
Honduras	1.4	14.8	2.1	9.4
Mexico	82.1	322.2	10.7	22.5
Nicaragua	0.6	10.1	1.0	11.7
Panama	0.1	2.8	0.3	2.3

Source: 1960 Data: U.N. *Yearbook of International Trade Statistics*, 1964 (New York: United Nations, 1966).

1969 Data: *U.N. Yearbook, 1969* (New York: United Nations, 1971).

In all cases the figures are computed from data on the individual countries' imports and exports by SITC code.

Americans would like to see and certainly does not indicate that growth in manufactures is playing a dominant role in the development of the Latin American economies.

As can be expected, the experience of the various countries differs considerably. Table 6-5 looks at the individual countries over the 1960-69 period in terms of their exports of manufactures. It can be seen that every country except the Dominican Republic increased the percentage share of manufactured exports. Once again the most dramatic increases came in the Central American countries (with the exception of Honduras). Their manufactured exports now range from Nicaragua's 11.7 percent to El Salvador's 31.1 percent, excluding Honduras with its 9.4 percent. But the increases in the rest of Latin America were also quite significant, though the resultant percentage of total trade in manufactures only reaches Argentina's high of 12.1 percent.

Another dimension of this development is that the role of the United States in receiving Latin American manufactured exports declined over the period. In

1960 the United States took 39.6 percent of these exports; by 1967 this percentage had fallen to 26.6 percent. The shift here was to intra-Latin American trade in manufactures, especially in the Central American Common Market. There has been some increase in manufactured exports to the United States, but it has been relatively small and concentrated in countries like Mexico. This is despite the rapid increase in imports of manufactures from the United States. This situation has resulted in an ever increasing deficit for Latin America in trade of this nature. She runs a bilateral surplus in trade of food, raw materials, and fuel, but this is more than offset by the deficit in manufactures.[9]

It is more difficult to assess the implications of those trends for the 1970s. While Latin America has never produced large amounts of manufactured goods for export, the combination of favorable exchange rates, trade preferences, and the activity of multinational firms may change this situation. At any rate, an important influence in this area will be the multinational enterprises and their effect on exports, a topic considered in more detail in the next section. At this point, all that can be said is that Latin American manufactured exports have increased and are likely to continue to do so, given supportive government policies and institutional developments.

Manufactured Exports and the Multinationals

While the 1960s saw significant shifts in the patterns of trade between the United States and Latin America, it has been noted above that a simple extrapolation of trends is likely to be unwarranted for a variety of reasons. The problem which must be examined at this point is what modifications in this pattern seem likely to play a major role during the 1970s. Of course, many factors might be selected, but the remainder of the paper will concentrate on the role of multinational firms, especially of United States origin, in the foreign trade of the Latin American nations. I have documented elsewhere the rapid growth of the United States version of the multinational enterprise, the "multinational conglomerates."[10] Similar growth is occurring with the firms of other countries, and much of it at this point is in the areas of the world termed "less developed." For example, Japanese firms invested $80.9 million in Latin America during 1970, most of it in Brazil and Mexico and most of it in manufacturing and natural resource industries.[11]

While the impact of these firms and their operations on balance of payments is direct and apparent, a more important effect for present purposes is that on the foreign trade of the Latin American nations. As yet little information is available on this question; however, the Department of Commerce has carried out two surveys which provide some appreciation of the trade operations of these firms.[12] The more recent survey came about mainly as a result of the furor over the Hartke-Burke bill, which would put severe restraints on multinationals. The Commerce Department surveyed a number of these firms to assess their effect on employment and on the imports and exports of the United States. This followed up an exhaustive 1966 study on these firms, the "benchmark survey."[13]

Table 6-6 gives some indication of the involvement of these firms in the export trade. On a worldwide scale, 30 percent of their production was exported in 1970. In Latin America about 27 percent of total production was exported, 17 percent to countries other than the United States. In Latin America in 1970 this means that the exports of these firms to the United States were $1.4 billion and to other countries $2.2 billion.[14]

It should be noted that the manufacturing companies have less of a tendency to export than do those in mining, trade, and petroleum. In 1970 they exported only 5 percent of their production, as compared with the 17 percent for all industries. This particular figure may be biased because of the sampling technique, as it would be in the interest of firms with large exports to the United States not to respond to the questionnaire. However, there does appear to be a significant difference across industries. Thus it can be seen that the United States multinationals in these countries do in general play a significant role in international trade as well as in domestic production. The role of such United States firms and those of other nationalities is likely to increase during the 1970s.

In order to gain a greater appreciation of the role of these firms, especially in

Table 6-6
Percentage of Sales of U.S. Multinational Subsidiaries Outside of Their Host Country[a]

Hosted in All Areas of World							
To U.S.				To Other Countries			
All Industries		Manufacturing		All Industries		Manufacturing	
1966	1970	1966	1970	1966	1970	1966	1970
.060	.066	.055	.079	.200	.230	.144	.160

Hosted in Latin America							
To U.S.				To Other Countries			
All Industries		Manufacturing		All Industries		Manufacturing	
1966	1970	1966	1970	1966	1970	1966	1970
.127	.105	NA	.02	.211	.166	NA	.03

[a]Disaggregated by location of subsidiary and destination of export sale.
Source: U.S. Department of Commerce, *Special Survey of US Multinational Companies, 1970* (Washington: National Technical Information Service, 1972).

the area of manufactured exports, we would like to examine their impact in two particular Latin American countries, Brazil and Mexico. There are several reasons for choosing these countries. First of all, only Venezuela is more important in overall Latin American trade and in that area's trade with the United States. While in 1971 Venezuela accounted for 25 percent of United States imports from the area, Mexico and Brazil together accounted for 35 percent. No other country had a share greater than 8 percent of the total Latin American exports to the United States.[15] But Venezuela is a special case, largely dependent on oil exports. Thus her relationship is likely to depend on United States energy policy and on her participation in the Organization of Petroleum Exporting Countries. The other two countries are more typical of Latin America and account for a significant portion of the total trade with the United States. Insights into their cases would be more likely to provide a basis for generalization.

A second aspect of their trade is the growth of their manufactured exports. Together they accounted for over 50 percent of Latin American manufactured exports in 1969. Their share of United States imports of manufactures from Latin America was still higher. With one exception due to classification problems, they accounted for between 65 percent and 95 percent of Latin American exports to the United States in the five categories of manufactured goods. The importance of this type of good both in trade and in development has been noted above.[16]

The final reason is the size and significance of the operations of multinationals in their economies. Brazil and Mexico will be seen to provide polar cases of the effect of multinationals. In at least one area of Mexico, the northern border area, the multinationals are playing a role very similar to that of other "export enclave" industries of the past in the developing economies, a role whose positive effect on development is not immediately obvious. In Brazil, however, the role is very different, with the effects on the economy much more likely to be beneficial. In both cases there are also effects on United States trade patterns.[17]

Brazil

Brazil is the third most important Latin American country in terms of value of trade with the United States. Her 1971 share of Latin American exports to the United States was 15 percent. During most of the 1960s, her position in total Latin American trade was also third; however, since the last years of the decade, she has been the second leading exporter, following Venezuela.

Certainly the primary reason for the growth in Brazil's importance is the active program of export stimulation undertaken by the Brazilian Revolutionary government after 1964. There are a large number of incentives available to exporters, including the waiving of some taxes, the waiving of import duties on machinery and components, access to the capital market, etc. One estimate claims that the incentives can lower product price by 52 percent.[18]

This is somewhat of a departure from previous Brazilian experience. Historically, her exports have been seen as an outlet for surplus production rather than an area of positive economic contribution. As such, they have generally been ignored or even discriminated against. Indeed, Leff finds that it was problems in the export sector brought about by poor government policy that caused the slowdown of the economy in 1964.[19]

The results of the government program of export promotion have been quite significant. According to official Brazilian statistics, there was only a 30 percent rise in her exports from 1960 to 1967, from $1.27 to $1.65 billion. But by 1969 exports had risen to $2.31 billion and unofficial estimates for 1972 put the amount at $3.8 billion, or more than double in five years. Apparently a large part of this increase has been in the manufactured goods area. Such goods were less than 10 percent of exports in 1967, but by 1972 they constituted 28 percent of exports. Government projections now see total exports rising to $8 billion by 1980.[20]

An interesting aspect of this growth is that the share of Brazil in United States imports of manufactures from Latin America had not risen appreciably by 1971. The total amount of such imports had risen, but in most cases not as fast as that from other Latin American countries.[21] The main market for Brazilian exports is the Latin American Free Trade Association. The share of LAFTA in her manufactured exports rose from 34 percent in 1963 to 70 percent in 1969.[22] From this impressive performance, it might seem that Brazil is following a classic pattern of growth through export promotion, manufactured exports in this case, and that her growth has little relevance to the United States. However, a closer examination indicates that foreign firms, particularly United States firms, play a major role in the Brazilian economy, both in the domestic economy and its international economic relations. For example, of the top 100 firms in Brazil in 1969, the public sector owned 63.4 percent, foreign private capital 24.7 percent, and Brazilian private capital only 11.9 percent.[23] In terms of United States private investment in Brazil, the book value of such investments increased from $953 to $1,843 million between 1960 and 1970. In manufacturing, investment increased from $515 to $1,247 million.[24] Thus, virtually all of the increase has come in manufacturing industries.

The presence and importance of foreign investment in Brazil in a time of rapidly increasing exports raises the question of the impact of these investors on Brazilian exports, and in particular on exports of manufactured products.

Direct evidence on the role of these firms is once again scanty, and so inferences from other types of data must be made. On the basis of such an effort, it does seem that foreign firms are playing a major role in the growth of exports. In several of the industries where there was sizeable investment, most of it new rather than reinvested earnings, there were substantial increases in exports during 1967-69. Examples are auto parts, whose exports more than doubled, and electrical apparatus, whose exports increased 79 percent. Textiles are a similar case, except that a higher percentage of the investment is reinvested profit, so the effect of new investment is not so likely.[25]

A second type of evidence is anecdotal. For example:

For Corning Glass, Brazil is the base for supplying picture tubes to Argentina; for IBM, Burroughs, Olivetti, RCA, and others, it is a base for millions of dollars worth of exports in office machines and electronic equipment to other LAFTA countries; for Kodak, Brazil is the base for supplying photographic paper to the region, while for 3-M it is the base for its small copying machine and possibly other products.[26]

The evidence of widespread participation is strong. It should be noted at this point that this involvement does raise a series of questions about the effect of these firms on Brazilian development. The usual assumption is that trade increases the welfare of the trading countries. But foreign ownership of the export capability raises a series of difficulties for the simple assumption of the benefit of trade. It is possible that the technique of production and its labor intensity or skill formation may be less appropriate than if a domestic firm were involved. Also the generation and disposition of capital might not be optimal from the national point of view. Thus an examination of the operations of foreign firms as compared with domestic firms is needed to assess the development effects of these firms.[27] Unfortunately, this paper can only give some indications as to the general mode of operation of United States multinationals in the import-export sphere.

To obtain direct information on the export effect of such firms, the author developed a questionnaire which was sent to United States capital goods firms with subsidiaries in Brazil. A series of questions was asked which would allow the assessment of the balance of payments effect of the operations of these firms. The size of the sample, fifty-five firms, and of the response, twenty-eight firms, makes any conclusions drawn very tentative.

The first thing noted by the questionnaire is that the experience of the firms varies quite dramatically. In some cases the firms have been in operation for up to twenty-eight years and are still not exporting any of their product. At the other extreme are the firms of recent origin which export up to 50 percent of their product.

The strongest pattern which appears is that of the established firm which then goes into the export market; 40 percent of the respondents followed this pattern. In these cases we find firms that were established in Brazil since the late 1950s, in most cases to begin production behind the import substitution tariff walls erected by the Brazilian government. Generally they had produced primarily for the domestic market and had eventually gotten most of their materials and some of their capital goods from Brazil. Then, in recent years, with the government's programs and the formation of LAFTA, they have become active in the export trade, generally by expanding their present plant facilities. Very little of their exports go to the United States, most going to LAFTA countries and some being exported to Europe. In these cases, the balance of trade and payments effect of these firms is quite direct. They are certainly helping the short-run Brazilian balance position, especially since they have minimal reliance on imported materials. This pattern is considered by Raymond Vernon as characteristic of the multinational enterprise.[28]

A second "grouping" of firms comprises 30 percent of the firms. These firms had been in operation in Brazil for a number of years, but had established subsidiaries which were directly involved in production for export. In some cases the product was similar to that of the parent company; but in most cases, it was a different product designed specifically for the export market. In general it was found that these subsidiaries were much more heavily reliant on imported capital goods and raw materials than the original firm. Thus their short run balance of payment effect was less apparently beneficial to Brazil. It should be noted that this pattern deviates from the "product cycle" hypothesis advanced by Vernon, though since the companies under investigation are not consumer goods companies for the most part, this may not be a major difficulty for that theory.[29]

Beyond these patterns, few regularities appear. It is generally the case that the newer firms are more involved in the export market than older firms, but there are exceptions. Thus on balance it does seem that an evaluation of these firms' operations in terms of their effect on trade and the Brazilian balance of payments must conclude that they have been beneficial. Of course, as noted above, this is but one aspect of their likely effect on the Brazilian economy.

Before moving to Mexico, a few words should be said about the implications of these operations for the United States. There seems little doubt that the type of involvement we have seen in Brazil will grow during the 1970s. More investments will be undertaken, and many more of these firms will export a portion of their production—if not to the United States, then to Latin America or Europe. Everyone seems to gain from this operation except the United States laborer, and his power is unlikely to be able to reverse this trend. Add to the effect of the United States firms' operations the likelihood that other countries producing in the same area will export their products to the United States, and we find that this may result in significant increases in Brazilian exports to the United States. Whether this will lead to the reversal of commodity trade noted above is open to question, but the tendency in this direction is strong.

Mexico

Mexico has a chronic imbalance in her trading accounts which is generally offset by her tourist receipts. In 1970 she had a total trade deficit of $1.1 billion, of which her deficit with the United States accounted for $730 million.[30] In 1958 her deficit with the United States was $309 million. This deficit is primarily in manufactured goods, as Mexico has a surplus in her trade of agricultural products with the United States. The overall deficit continues despite the doubling of Mexican exports to the United States during the 1960s.

Another significant aspect of U.S.-Mexican economic relations has been the growth of United States foreign investment over the same period. As measured by book values, total United States direct investment in Mexico increased from $795 million in 1960 to $1,774 million in 1970. By far the most rapidly increasing investment was in manufacturing industries, which had a rise in book value from $391 to $1,191 million.[31]

Examination of Mexican export performance during the 1960s shows that her overall exports increased at a rate of 6.2 percent per year. On the other hand, between 1962 and 1969 her manufactured exports increased at an annual rate of 19.8 percent. They accounted for 27 percent of her 1969 exports and for over 50 percent of the increase in exports between 1962 and 1969.[32] This is a creditable performance, but juxtaposing this information with that of the increase in United States foreign investment raises again the question of the role of United States firms in this trade. An examination of this question will be the focus of this section, and particular attention will be paid to the "border industries," the United States role in them, and their effect on Mexican exports of manufactures.

In 1965 Mexico set up along her northern border with the United States a program which allowed firms to operate within 20 kilometers of the border under very different conditions from those in the rest of Mexico. Such firms are called "border industries."[33] They could import machinery and raw materials duty free, and they were exempt from most federal taxes and could be exempted from state taxes. The only stipulation was that the products of these firms could not be sold in Mexico but would have to be exported, primarily to the United States. In this fashion Mexico was able to take advantage of sections 807 and 806.3 of the United States Tariff Code, which with certain stipulations allow payment of tariffs on only the value added during processing in the foreign country. Thus Mexicans will receive the wages generated in this assembly work, United States firms will be able to take advantage of low cost Mexican labor, and presumably products in the United States will be cheaper for the procedure.

The firms are of interest for several reasons. First of all, since all of their output is exported, their effect on exports is much more easily isolated than is generally the case. Secondly, they serve to highlight one pole of the effect of multinationals on growth and development, the pole toward the "export enclave." By this is meant that the firms operate in isolation from the rest of the economy, and that as a result the beneficial effects which they should have on economic growth and development are not transmitted to the rest of the economy, but remain localized in their geographical area.[34]

Looking more closely at the problem at hand, we can see that the operation of these firms will have a number of effects on the Mexican international position. In the first instance there should be an improvement in her balance of payments, as she will receive a net gain in foreign exchange equal to the amount of value added in Mexico. However, to assess the full effect of the operations, it is necessary to take account of a number of other influences on Mexican trade and balance of payments. For example, a good portion of the wages generated in production are in turn spent on goods from the United States. One estimate places this at up to 80 percent of wages.[35] This would of course offset that portion of the exchange receipts. Other questions of relevance for which there is no empirical evidence are the degree to which this type of production is substituting for Mexican exports or the extent to which Mexican components are being excluded from this production by the operation of these plants.[36] The effect on capital flows should also be brought into consideration as a balance of payments factor, though capital investment tends to be small in these industries.

Finally, full consideration requires an evaluation of the overall impact of border industries on the Mexican economy. They seem likely to produce a high wage sector cut off from the rest of the economy, generating some foreign exchange, but not of the sort that could fuel a major development effort. They also may be affecting consumption patterns—in the area and in the rest of Mexico—in a fashion not in accord with development needs. Also, while they are transmitting labor skills, the type of skill is once again unlikely to provide a motive force for development.[37] As noted above, the 1960s saw a significant increase in exports from Mexico, and of more direct interest, in exports of manufactured products. The question at hand is the role of the border industry operations on this pattern.

Table 6-7 presents an overview of the operation of these firms. The first thing to note is that the growth of the number of firms in the border industries has been quite rapid. There were 46 such plants in operation by 1968. By 1970 the number had increased to 165 authorized plants, with 120 in operation. Authorizations then accelerated, reaching 293 by June of 1971 and 345 by June of 1972. If three-fourths of those authorized were in operation, the number of firms in operation would have been 260 by June of 1972. In addition to the rapid growth in authorizations along the Northern Border, the government of Mexico has extended the areas where such plants can operate to all coastlines of the Republic. The exports of these firms increased from $7 million to $150 million between 1966 and 1969. Another aspect of the border industries which will be of some importance is that textiles, electronics, and toys account for over 70 percent of their ouput. Of these, by far the most important industry is electronics.[38]

The other information necessary at this point is the general development of Mexican trade with the United States. (See Table 6-8.) It will be seen that the composition of Mexico's trade with the United States has changed quite

Table 6-7
The Operations of the "Border Industries" of Mexico

	Value of Exports of Mexican Border Industries, 1969 (thousands of dollars)		
	Total Value	Value Added	% Value Added
Total	150012	52124	34.7
Total (807)	145212	49424	34.0
Textiles	17078	4407	25.8
Electronics	94170	29582	31.4
Toys	17267	8457	49.0
Scientific Instruments	5574	4330	77.7
Other (magnetic tape; wood products)	11123	2378	21.4
Total (806.3)			
(automobile parts; metal hoops; electronic components)	4800	2700	56.3

Source: Banco Nacional de Comerico Exterior, *Comercio Exterior*, (Mexico: Banco Nacional de Comercio Exterior), May 1970.

	Number of Authorized Firms in Border Area	
	June 1971	June 1972
Textiles	77	76
Electronics	118	152
Metal Manufacturers	26	22
Furniture	16	20
Leather	6	12
Plastic	6	10
Other	44	53
Total	293	345

Source: U.S. House of Representatives, Foreign Affairs Subcommittee on Interamerican Affairs, *U.S.-Mexican Trade Relations* (Washington: U.S. Government Printing Office, 1972).

significantly since 1960. Foods rose very rapidly until 1971, when there were agreements between the governments to restrict exports such as strawberries. The other primary categories (1-4) were very sluggish, in one case (3) dropping significantly. On the other hand chemicals (5) grew over the decade, but only in the earlier years. Category 9 also grew slowly over the period. So the major growth occurred in groups 6-8, and particularly in group 8. As noted above, these are the groups where the border industries are concentrated. Thus, as a first approximation we might suggest that their growth had a major role in the growth of manufactured exports from Mexico. Looking at the data at a bit more disaggregated level only strengthens this initial impression.

Table 6-8
Structure of Mexico's Exports to the U.S. (thousands of dollars)

	SITC	1960	1967	1970	1971
Foods	(0)	243,371	362,777	573,655	556,058
Beverages	(1)	1,903	5,354	7,570	8,946
Crude Materials	(2)	5,243	100,216	109,835	96,511
Mineral Fuel	(3)	47,021	66,459	61,324	27,250
Oil and Fat	(4)	9,971	2,063	1,444	2,013
Chemicals	(5)	9,347	40,444	24,902	27,285
Manufactures by Chief Material	(6)	61,393	86,092	120,312	149,511
Machinery	(7)	922	14,073	153,735	200,602
Misc. Manufacturing	(8)	34,819	23,699	99,094	114,849
Not Classified	(9)	24,751	47,715	70,517	79,464
Total		445,171	748,895	1,222,392	1,262,489

Source: U.S. Department of Commerce, *US General Imports: World Area by Commodity Grouping* (Washington: U.S. Government Printing Office, 1961-72).

Examination of the increase in manufactured exports to the United States between 1967 and 1971, the period of their most rapid increase and the period of the operation of the border industries, shows that of the $327,939,000 increase in exports in categories 5-8, over $289,000,000 or 86 percent was accounted for by industries in which the border industry firms were active: metal manufactures, electronics, vehicle parts, clothing, toys, and musical instruments.

The question is what the role of the border firms was in this increase. An indication can be gotten by comparing the figures for production in these industries in 1970 with the increase in production in the relevant industries between 1967 and 1970. The two digit industries of interest increased their exports by $233,375,000 between 1967 and 1970. At the same time the Tariff Commission Report found an increase in production by the 807 and 806.3 firms of $143,000,000. Thus the high estimate is that 60 percent of the increase in imports of Mexican consumer goods into the United States came from border industries. This is somewhat of an overestimate, for a portion of the production is exported to other countries and thus would not appear in the United States import figures. Also, there is some difficulty in assigning industries to trade categories. Although these difficulties may lower the share of the border industries, it is unlikely that they accounted for less than 50 percent of the increase in the exports of manufactured products in the classes noted.

While this highlights the importance of the border industries for Mexico's trade with the United States, in the scope of total Mexican manufactured exports it is possible that their importance would be greatly diminished. However, this is not the case, as data from the *Yearbook of International Trade Statistics* on total Mexican exports indicate. Mexico's exports of manufactured goods in 1969 were $322 million, but with SITC category 68 added, they were around $428.6 million. There was actually a drop in the amount of these exports during 1966-67, but since then there has been a very rapid rise. Taking the higher figure of $430 million and comparing it with the total output of the border industries, it appears that over 34 percent of all of Mexico's manufactured exports come from the border industries. Thus the conclusion drawn concerning the importance of these industries for U.S.-Mexican trade can be expanded into a conclusion about their importance for total Mexican export of manufactured goods.

It seems likely that the growth of the border industries will continue, but at a diminished pace. The government of Mexico is definitely committed to such a program, and it is discovering that Europe and Japan have tariff treatment of assembled goods similar to that of the United States. There may be some additional barriers to their growth in the United States trade, however. President Nixon's trade message singled out this type of firm as subject to changes in tax laws whereby, for instance, earnings may be taxed when earned rather than when repatriated. While this might tend to eliminate some firms, evidence seems to indicate that the advantages of these operations are of such magnitude that major revisions in tax and tariff treatment would be necessary to slow their growth.

Several propositions have emerged from this consideration of the Mexican case.

1. There has been very rapid growth in exports of manufactures from Mexico, and the United States multinational firms operating along the border with the United States have played a major role in this growth, their exports accounting for over one-third of total Mexican manufactured exports in 1970.

2. At present there are few links between the border areas and the rest of the country, though the Mexican government is attempting to implement a series of policies which can affect the "enclave" nature of the border industries and can ensure that their benefits are transmitted to the rest of the economy.

3. The prospects for future growth of these firms seem good, though several factors may alter this. The Mexican government is interested in expanding this type of firm and will pursue policies in accordance with this goal. The United States government, however, is ponderously moving toward putting some pressures on the firms, though it is unlikely that presently contemplated policies will have much effect. Finally, of course, other countries are competing with Mexico for the firms and it is possible that growth will be slowed for this reason.[39]

A Summary Look at the 1970s

The information presented in this chapter documents quite clearly the decline in the importance of the United States and of Latin America to each other's trade.

However, all of the present indicators are that this decline should slow and perhaps even reverse itself. At the same time, there may be some interesting reversals in the types of commodities exported by the two partners. It is entirely conceivable that by 1980 the Latin American countries will have a net surplus in their trade of manufactures with the United States, while the United States will be supplying much of their agricultural imports. This pattern does not result simply from the recent growth of United States agricultural exports, but policies in both areas as well as institutional structures are increasing pressure in this direction.

The final area of relevance for the 1970s is some insight into the role of multinationals, particularly United States multinationals in trade patterns. It is clearly evident that these firms already play a major role in the exports of manufactured products from the Latin American countries investigated. It is also apparent that their role will increase apace with investment during the 1970s. This chapter has raised a number of questions about the effect of the operations of these firms, first in the international trade area, but even more so in the area of the development of the countries in which they are involved. At one extreme it was found that the benefits of the countries beyond the trade area are minimal and perhaps even negative, at the other extreme it seems that there may be more substantial benefits, benefits which should be measured more clearly.

Notes

1. A good treatment of United States investment in Latin America is Marvin Bernstein, ed., *Foreign Investment in Latin America* (New York: Knopf, 1966). Data on trade with the United States are contained in various volumes of U.S. Bureau of the Census, *Summary of Foreign Commerce of the US* (Washington: U.S. Government Printing Office, various years). Actually as late as 1949, over 40 percent of United States imports came from Latin America.

2. In this regard it is interesting to note that the Latin American countries have generally maintained basically the same exchange rate *vis-à-vis* the dollar during the various dollar devaluations. When combined with the United States devaluation against Europe and Japan, this may serve to alter the declining trend in Latin American importance in United States imports.

3. This differential importance plays a major role in the "dependency" model used to describe the international position of the Latin American countries. See for example Barbara Stallings, *Economic Dependency in Africa and Latin America* (Berkeley, Calif.: Sage, 1972); Susanne Bodenheimer, "Dependency and Imperialism: The Roots of Latin American Underdevelopment," *Politics and Society*, vol. 1, May 1971, pp. 327-357; and Oswaldo Sunkel, "National Development Policy and External Dependence in Latin America," *Journal of Development Studies*, vol. 6, October 1969, pp. 23-48.

4. The Central American Common Market (CACM) is composed of Costa Rica, El Salvador, Guatemala, Honduras, and Nicaragua. The Latin American Free Trade Association (LAFTA) is composed of Argentina, Bolivia, Brazil, Colombia, Chile, Ecuador, Mexico, Paraguay, Peru, Uruguay, and Venezuela. The Andean Group (ANCOM) is a subgrouping of LAFTA composed of Bolivia, Colombia, Chile, Ecuador, Peru and Venezuela.

5. For an interesting treatment of the historical causes of this situation, see Barbara Stein and Stanley Stein, *The Colonial Heritage of Latin America* (New York: Oxford University Press, 1970).

6. The exchange rate adjustments have already been mentioned. Additional evidence on this point comes from Table 6-2, in which the patterns appearing during most of the 1960s are quite weak or even non-existent in the later years of the decade.

7. The Central American Common Market has run into a number of difficulties recently with the continuing feud between Honduras and El Salvador. This has severely disrupted trade within the community and may cause a reorientation toward the United States until the political problems can be solved. This may be another offsetting factor in the decline in U.S.-L.A. trade.

8. The figures in these sections were computed from data in United Nations, Economic Commission for Latin America, *Economic Survey of Latin America, 1970* (New York: United Nations, 1972).

9. It is an interesting possibility for the 1970s that this situation may reverse itself. The United States is now rapidly increasing its agriculture exports. At the same time Latin America is increasing her manufactured exports, and as multinationals continue to expand their production in Latin America and their exports from those countries, it is not at all unlikely that this pattern could be reversed.

10. Kenneth Jameson, "The Castle or the Tipi: Rationalization or Irrationality in the American Economy," in Ronald Weber, ed., *America in Change* (Notre Dame, Ind.: University of Notre Dame Press, 1972), pp. 13-25.

11. Oriental Economist, *Japan Economic Yearbook*, 1971 (Tokyo: The Toyo kelzai shimpo sha Ltd., 1972).

12. The data are contained in the mimeographed publication by the Department of Commerce, "Special Survey of US Multinational Companies, 1970" (Washington: National Technical Information Service, 1972).

13. There are a number of severe problems with the more recent survey as carried out. It was voluntary and thus only 298 of the 455 enterprises polled actually answered the request for data. It is likely that those omitted would come out worse if measured against the Hartke-Burke bill. Also, even the 455 would have comprised only 14 percent of all the "multinational firms" included in the 1966 benchmark survey carried out by the Commerce Department.

14. Assuming representativeness of these firms, some inferences about their overall role can be made. Total sales of these subsidiaries in Latin America were

$13.1 billion in 1970. Using the direct investment figures and a very rough approximation given in the Department of Commerce Study, Part III, p. 19, we can estimate that total affiliate sales were $35 billion. Thus the sample would cover 37 percent of total sales. Total sales by the affiliates to the United States, if proportionality existed, would be $3.8 billion, and to other countries would be $5.9 billion. This would be 48 percent of the total Latin American exports as reported in the U.N. *Statistical Bulletin for Latin America*, 1971 (New York: United Nations, 1972). This estimate is higher than that for Mexico quoted in U.S. House of Representatives, who found that United States firms accounted for 33 percent of Mexico's exports during 1965-68 (U.S. Congress, Foreign Affairs Subcommittee on Interamerican Affairs, "U.S.-Mexican Trade Relations," Washington: U.S. Government Printing Office, 1972), p. 17.

15. Data used in this section were computed from U.N. Economic Commission for Latin America, *Economic Survey of Latin America* (New York: United Nations, various issues) and from U.S. Department of Commerce, *Imports of the US by World Area and Commodity Grouping* (Washington: U.S. Government Printing Office, 1972).

16. A significant recent survey of the role of manufactured exports in the LDCs, and of the situation of Mexico and Brazil, is given in Gerald Helleiner, "Manufactured Exports from Less-Developed Countries and Multinational Firms," *The Economic Journal*, vol. 83, March 1973, pp. 21-47.

17. Of course the effects of these firms are quite broad and are a matter of some controversy. Their impact on trade may not be their crucial impact. Their impact on ownership and control and on profit generation may be of greater import to all the economies. However, the matter which has been the object of most concern recently, especially with United States labor, is the impact of these firms on U.S. trade patterns and production. For good treatments of many of the dimensions of the multinational, see Jere Behrman, *National Interests and Multinational Enterprises* (Englewood Cliffs, N.J.: Prentice-Hall, 1970) or Raymond Vernon, *Sovereignty at Bay* (New York: Basic Books, 1971).

18. Business International Corporation, *Brazil: New Business Power in Latin America* (New York: Business International Corporation, 1971), p. 40.

19. Nathaniel Leff, "Export Stagnation and Autarkic Development in Brazil, 1947-1962," *The Quarterly Journal of Economics*, vol. 81, May 1967, pp. 286-301.

20. Earlier years' data are taken from Instituto Brasileiro de Estatistica, *Anuario Estatistico do Brasil*, 1970 (Rio de Janeiro: Fundacao IBGE, 1970). More recent information is from Visao, *Brazil Report, 1973* (Sao Paulo: Visao, 1973). Recently some questions have been raised as to whether the government's finance ministry might be overstating export figures, particularly of coffee, to increase domestic popularity, see Latin America Newsletter, *Latin America*, vol. 7, July 27, 1973, p. 1.

21. To give an indication of the importance of Brazil for U.S. manufactured

imports in 1970, we find her share of total imports from Latin America to be the following: chemicals: 17.2 percent; manufactured goods by material: 7.5 percent; machinery: 3.6 percent; miscellaneous manufactures: 7.7 percent. Thus Brazil is not very important except in chemicals, and within chemicals she is important only in chemical elements and compounds (51) and perfumes and oils (55).

22. Business International Corporation, op. cit., p. 41. Visao, op. cit., uses a figure of 60 percent. It should be noted that Latin America takes only 12 percent of all Brazilian exports.

23. Business International Corporation, op. cit., p. 9. Visao, op. cit., p. 66, indicates that in 1973 foreign firms controlled 20 percent of the top 1,000 firms.

24. U.S. Department of Commerce, *Survey of Current Business*, vol. 41, August 1961, pp. 22-23; vol. 52, November 1972, pp. 28-29.

25. Investment data are from Business International Corporation, op. cit., and trade data are from *Instituto Brasileiro de Estatistica*, op. cit.

26. Business International Corporation, op. cit., p. 41. Similarly Visao, op. cit., p. 65, indicates that IBM was exporting $70 million worth of equipment yearly and had embarked in 1972 on a $857 million export project in Japan.

27. Issues such as these have been considered in greater depth by Professor Cohen in Chapter 5 of this volume. At least for his countries and companies, he finds little significant difference on a number of these items.

28. Raymond Vernon, op. cit.

29. Raymond Vernon, ibid., Ch. 3.

30. Kenneth Ruddle and Mukhtar Hamour, eds., *Statistical Abstract of Latin America, 1970* (Los Angeles: University of California Press, 1971), p. 322.

31. U.S. Department of Commerce, *Survey of Current Business*, vol. 41, August 1961, pp. 22-23; vol. 52, November 1972, pp. 28-29.

32. Helleiner, op. cit., p. 24.

33. Rudolfo Villarreal C., "Industrialization of Mexico's Northern Border and the United States Investor," *Arizona Review*, vol. 17, January 1968, pp. 6-9.

34. For an exposition of this model, see Jonathan Levin, *The Export Economies* (Cambridge, Mass.: Harvard University Press, 1960), or Robert Baldwin, "Export Technology and Development from a Subsistence Level," *Economic Journal*, vol. 73, March 1963, pp. 80-92.

35. David Tansik and Humberto Tapia S., "Is the Twin Plants Concept in Trouble?" *Arizona Review*, vol. 19, December 1970, pp. 6-12.

36. The U.S. Tariff Commission carried out a study of these plants in 1970 and recommended their continuation. One point they made is that their elimination throughout the world would be likely to worsen the United States trade balance by $150-$250 million. Implicit in their estimate is the assumption that overseas production would continue, but use foreign components. This seems to overstate the case. See U.S. Tariff Commission, *Economic Factors*

Affecting the Use of Items 807.00 and 806.30 of the Tariff Schedules of the United States (Washington: U.S. Tariff Commission, September 1970).

37. General treatments of the effect of the operation of these firms are given in Anna Ericson, "An Analysis of Mexico's Border Industrialization Program," *Monthly Labor Review*, vol. 93, May 1970, pp. 33-40, and Raul Fernandez, "The Border Industrial Program on the United States-Mexico Border," *Review of Radical Political Economy*, vol. 5, Spring 1973, pp. 37-52. An interesting aspect of the skill development is that rural peasants can be trained readily for work in the firms; Cohen notes the same phenomenon in Asia. This can be interpreted in two ways: either the peasants have innate abilities generally underestimated, or the skills imparted are rudimentary, requiring little sophistication. This latter interpretation would be consistent with the export enclave model.

38. U.S. Tariff Commission, op. cit., U.S. House of Representatives, Foreign Affairs Subcommittee on Interamerican Affairs, "U.S.-Mexican Trade Relations," (Washington: U.S. Government Printing Office, 1972).

39. Gerald Helleiner, op. cit., sees this as a major limitation on the growth of these firms in any country.

7

Trade with the Soviet Union and Eastern Europe

Roger Skurski
University of Notre Dame

Introduction

During the last decade a number of important changes have occurred in the Soviet Union and Eastern Europe and in the relations of these countries with the rest of the world, particularly the United States. Despite the invasion of Czechoslovakia in 1968, these countries continue to be open to change at least within broadly defined limits, the most crucial of which seems to be the degree of power of the Communist Party. After the Yugoslav break with Stalin at the end of the 1940s and the Sino-Soviet Rift in 1960, it was no longer appropriate to speak of world communism as a single system; but today with the popularization of the idea that there is more than one path to communism, one should take cognizance of the variety of experiences in the USSR and East Europe. Internally, all of the economies of this area have undergone economic reform of their systems of management and planning, and these too, differ from country to country in variety and degree.[1] These factors, as well as the increasing detente with the West, may have influenced the foreign trade of this group of countries in rather important ways.

It is the purpose of this chapter to analyze the development of Soviet and East European foreign trade since 1950 in light of these changes, with special attention being given to trade with the United States. Overall growth of trade, its geographic distribution, and its commodity composition will be examined first, followed by a discussion of American economic relationships with the Soviet Union and its economic partners. We will conclude with a discussion of the trade problems currently facing the Eastern European countries in general, and with the United States in particular.

Patterns of Trade

The Council for Mutual Economic Assistance (CEMA or CMEA or Comecon) was established in 1949 to counter the influence of the Marshall Plan in Europe and to provide a vehicle for the collective solution of problems facing the countries of East Europe at that time. The original members were Bulgaria, Czechoslovakia, Hungary, Poland, Rumania, and the Soviet Union. When East Germany joined shortly afterward, the full active membership was complete. I will direct my attention to these seven countries, since until very recently all other countries associated with CEMA possessed only observer status.

The influence of foreign economic relations on the Soviet economy as measured by the ratio of trade to national income has been and continues to be rather small, although it has been rising; this is similar to the American experience, as Professor Rakowski has pointed out in his chapter. The size, structure, and resource endowments of these economies help to explain this, but in the Soviet case it has also been the result of a conscious policy of pursuing as large a measure of self-sufficiency as possible. However, since 1950 the role of foreign trade has markedly increased in the USSR, and also in the other countries of East Europe, where the strategy of autarky was much less feasible in any case. Table 7-1 presents the overall picture of the growth of Soviet and East

Table 7-1
CEMA Foreign Trade: Average Annual Growth (percent)

	1951-55	1956-60	1961-65	1966-71
		Exports		
Bulgaria	15.3	19.7	15.6	10.8
Czechoslovakia	8.7	10.6	6.8	7.7
East Germany	28.7	11.6	6.9	8.7
Hungary	12.9	9.5	11.6	8.8
Poland	7.8	7.7	10.9	9.7
Rumania	14.9	12.1	8.9	11.4
USSR	14.1	10.4	8.1	9.1
CEMA Total	13.7	10.4	8.6	9.1
		Imports		
Bulgaria	14.1	22.0	13.3	10.6
Czechoslovakia	11.4	11.7	8.1	7.1
East Germany	20.5	13.4	5.2	10.1
Hungary	12.1	13.9	9.4	12.3
Poland	8.2	10.2	9.4	9.5
Rumania	14.8	8.1	11.2	12.0
USSR	16.8	12.9	7.4	7.6
CEMA Total	14.0	12.4	7.9	8.8

Sources: Computed from Paul Marer, *Soviet and East European Foreign Trade, 1946-1969: A Statistical Compendium and Guide* (Bloomington: University of Indiana Press, 1972) pp. 24-44: 1946-69. International Development Research Center, University of Indiana, "Soviet and East European Trade Data Bank: 1970-71" (unpublished statistical material).

European foreign trade over the last two decades. The average yearly growth over the entire period was 10.4 percent (for exports), which is more than 25 percent higher than the growth of world exports over a similar period, and also higher than the growth of national income in the area of this period. Since the United Nations figures include CEMA trade, the difference between the rest of the world and these countries would be somewhat larger.[2] The world growth was also exceeded by each of the seven CEMA countries over this span. However, CEMA's share of world trade is still relatively small: about 10 percent compared to 28 percent for EEC, 14 percent for the United States, and about the same for EFTA.[3]

As the table shows, CEMA trade grew fastest in the early 1950s, but has slowed considerably since then. The growth of world commerce, on the other hand, has been accelerating and now is slightly higher than the CEMA rate. The increase in CEMA trade was slowest in the first half of the 1960s, which was a period of considerable internal economic difficulty for almost all of the centrally planned economies.

Despite the decreasing emphasis on individual country self-sufficiency, the CEMA group led by Stalin attempted to minimize the extent of its dependence on the world capitalist market by creating a parallel world democratic or socialist market. It was felt that this new market could provide every country with everything necessary for its economic development; but trade with the West was not excluded, since at times it could prove mutually beneficial. However, it was suggested that this interbloc trade was more important to the West, which could use it to relieve itself of its pressing surpluses.[4] Tables 7-2 and 7-3 show the significant degree to which the goal of a world socialist market was achieved. By 1953 more than 80 percent of Soviet and East European trade was with socialist countries, about 65 percent of the total being trade between the CEMA nations themselves, and the other 15 percent being almost entirely with China (trade with Yugoslavia after the split with the Soviet bloc was not resumed until 1954 and did not amount to much for the first year or so).[5] This development necessitated a complete reorientation of Soviet and East European trade, because prior to World War II all of these countries traded primarily with the developed economies of Western Europe and *not* with each other.[6] In fact according to Professor Spulber,

it can be asserted that on the whole, up to 1951, the Soviet Union seems to have viewed Eastern Europe as a limited "subsidiary" market mainly for the export of her industrial raw materials and the import of metals and manufactured goods—the last purchased in the ordinary way—or for the export of Russian raw material to be processed and re-exported by the East European countries.[7]

From the data presented here, it can be seen that Comecon has continued to emphasize trade with socialist countries, but the relative share of this kind of trade has diminished, so that now it accounts for 65-70 percent of the bloc's

Table 7-2

Exports of CEMA Countries (excluding Albania) (millions of current dollars[a], F.O.B., Except Hungary, C.I.F.)

Year	CEMA		Other CPEs[b] and Yugoslavia		MDCs[c]		LDCs[d]		Total
	Value	Percent	Value	Percent	Value	Percent	Value	Percent	Value
1950	2534.8	59.3	534.5	12.5	1016.1	23.8	154.3	3.6	4271.9
1952	3996.5	65.7	761.9	12.5	1077.2	17.7	214.5	3.5	6085.1
1953	4400.6	64.9	1063.0	15.7	1063.7	15.7	193.5	2.8	6784.7
1954	4637.3	62.0	1217.2	16.3	1244.4	16.6	298.2	4.0	7485.1
1955	4732.5	58.6	1251.8	15.5	1508.9	18.7	464.1	5.7	8075.9
1956	4772.6	55.3	1335.1	15.5	1704.5	19.7	657.8	7.6	8633.9
1957	5876.2	59.9	1208.4	12.3	1871.0	19.1	741.6	7.6	9817.2
1958	5958.6	57.8	1506.4	14.6	1946.5	18.9	900.0	8.7	10311.6
1959	7275.4	59.5	1801.2	14.7	2289.3	18.7	857.3	7.0	12223.2
1960	7994.2	60.6	1742.1	13.2	2599.7	19.7	852.6	6.5	13188.5
1961	8899.5	62.2	1912.6	9.9	2835.4	19.8	1166.3	8.1	14313.8
1962	10130.2	63.6	1317.3	8.3	2887.5	18.1	1603.0	10.1	15938.1
1963	10995.0	64.0	1403.2	8.2	3234.3	18.8	1539.4	9.0	17172.0
1964	11919.4	64.0	1446.3	7.8	3547.3	19.1	1705.8	9.2	18618.7
1965	12417.2	62.2	1557.6	7.8	4012.6	20.1	1960.4	9.8	19947.8
1966	12489.4	59.1	1919.2	9.1	4589.8	21.5	2149.5	10.2	21147.9
1967	13677.0	59.3	2049.4	8.9	5000.5	21.7	2326.9	10.1	23054.0
1968	15167.5	60.3	2305.1	9.2	5287.6	21.0	2401.4	9.5	25161.6
1969	16525.7	59.5	2358.1	8.5	6079.2	21.9	2817.8	10.1	27781.0
1970	18311.1	59.2	2571.5	8.3	6723.4	21.7	3287.3	10.6	30892.6
1971	19952.4	59.1	2895.6	8.5	7469.4	22.1	3401.8	10.0	33719.1

[a]Converted from national devisa units through official exchange rates. Limitations are noted in Marer's text.

[b]CPEs = Centrally Planned Economies: Mainly China, Cuba (since 1960), North Viet Nam.

[c]MDCs = More Developed Countries: North America, West Europe, South Africa, Japan and Oceania with some variations as between CEMA countries.

[d]LDCs = Less Developed Countries: Basically all other countries.

Sources: Marer, p. 43: 1950-69.

International Development Research Center "Soviet and East European Trade Data Bank: 1970-71."

total trade. Intrabloc trade has not exhibited such a long run decline, but instead has fluctuated at around 60 percent of the total. On the other hand, the group's trade with other centrally planned economies and Yugoslavia *has* fallen off in the last ten years to less than one-half of its previous level, and this is explained principally by the reduction of trade with the Chinese after 1960. This trade seems to have been replaced by trade with the West, which now purchases about

Table 7-3
Imports of CEMA Countries (excluding Albania) (millions of current dollars[a],
F.O.B., except Hungary, C.I.F.)

Year	CEMA		Other CPEs[b] and Yugoslavia		MDCs[c]		LDCs[d]		Total
	Value	Percent	Value	Percent	Value	Percent	Value	Percent	Value
1950	2464.6	62.8	289.4	7.37	941.2	23.98	185.7	4.73	3924.6
1952	3866.6	64.8	624.4	10.5	1169.6	19.6	250.0	4.2	5962.6
1953	4349.8	67.2	746.0	11.5	1122.1	17.3	196.7	3.0	6477.6
1954	4507.9	62.8	872.9	12.2	1386.5	19.3	333.2	4.6	7183.1
1955	4464.9	59.6	1016.2	13.6	1413.4	18.9	477.7	6.4	7490.1
1956	4706.0	56.7	1204.4	14.5	1684.5	20.3	530.7	6.4	8292.6
1957	5588.6	57.5	1241.5	12.8	2015.7	20.7	697.3	7.2	9717.1
1958	5795.8	57.3	1468.9	14.5	2059.3	20.4	791.9	7.8	10115.9
1959	7011.2	58.5	1801.2	15.0	2302.4	19.2	871.0	7.3	11986.7
1960	7834.5	58.5	1699.5	12.7	2877.3	21.5	978.4	7.3	13389.7
1961	8605.5	60.2	1523.3	10.7	3125.0	21.9	1041.2	7.3	14295.0
1962	9965.5	63.5	1392.8	8.9	3249.9	20.7	1084.7	6.9	15692.9
1963	10687.5	63.7	1279.1	7.6	3483.7	20.7	1225.6	7.3	16789.6
1964	11657.5	62.7	1327.9	7.1	4331.7	23.3	1280.2	6.9	18596.7
1965	12220.5	62.2	1496.8	7.6	4346.7	22.1	1592.0	8.1	19656.4
1966	12424.8	60.3	1410.9	6.8	5105.5	24.8	1673.9	8.1	20615.1
1967	13700.4	62.2	1403.6	6.4	5430.9	24.6	1498.8	6.8	22033.7
1968	15076.7	63.0	1331.3	5.6	5859.2	24.5	1659.9	6.9	23927.1
1969	16434.6	62.4	1311.6	5.0	6653.5	25.2	1953.5	7.4	26353.0
1970	18331.1	60.6	1773.7	5.8	7815.2	25.8	2258.1	7.4	30177.8
1971	20027.4	61.2	1837.6	5.6	7603.4	23.2	3229.7	9.8	32698.0

[a]Converted from national devisa units through official exchange rates. Limitations are noted in Marer's text.
[b]CPEs = Centrally Planned Economies: Mainly China, Cuba (since 1960), North Viet Nam.
[c]MDCs = More Developed Countries: North America, West Europe, South Africa, Japan and Oceania with some variations as between CEMA countries.
[d]LDCs = Less Developed Countries: Basically all other countries.

Sources: Marer, p. 33: 1950-69.
International Development Research Center "Soviet and East European Trade Data Bank, 1970-71."

22 percent of CEMA's exports and ships CEMA about a quarter of its imports, and by trade with less developed countries, whose share of the group's trade is still small (8-10 percent), but has risen significantly in recent years. The net imports of the bloc from the more developed countries have been more or less offset by its net export position with respect to the LDCs. This situation, no doubt, has much to do with the quality and mix of the products traded by the Soviet Union and East Europe.

In Table 7-4 we have summarized the available information on the commodity composition of CEMA foreign trade classified by the CEMA Trade Nomenclature (CTN), which is somewhat different from the Standard International Trade Classification (SITC) system used until recently by the United Nations. As can be seen, CEMA has experienced some shifts in the composition of its foreign trade since the time of Stalin: the principal ones being a greater share of trade in manufactured goods, both industrial and consumer types, and a reduced share for raw materials, fuels, and metals, with other divisions holding rather constant. Although raw materials and other Division II items continue to account for the largest single share of CEMA exports, in recent years CEMA has been importing as much machinery and equipment as raw materials, fuels, and so on.

Since Division I and IV contain only one category of goods each, I will not comment any further on them except to note that CEMA is still a net importer in both. Turning to Division II, on the export side the secular decline was concentrated in the fuel, mineral, animal, and vegetable raw material categories, while the export of chemicals actually rose somewhat. On the import side chemicals and building and construction materials stayed fairly constant as the other categories declined. Within Division III, on the export side there has been little overall change: a drop in raw materials for the production of food was offset by a rise in food exports; on the import side there has been a rather continuous decline contributed to by both major categories, the net result being that although the area continues to experience difficulties (more or less cyclically) in the agricultural sector, at the end of the 1960s it was on balance a net exporter of food and food materials. The portion of trade not specified presumably contains a large element of military equipment and supplies; and CEMA continues as a net exporter here, even though imports have been rising more rapidly than exports.

In summary, at the end of the 1960s CEMA was a net exporter of fuels, raw materials, foods, and probably defense materials, and a net importer of industrial machinery and equipment as well as industrial consumer products. Given the resource endowment and sectoral structure of these economies, we would expect this pattern to continue through the 1970s, except in those years when climatic conditions hinder agricultural output levels and force the bloc to become a net importer of food.

United States Trade with CEMA

Trade between the United States and the CEMA group historically has been of minor importance to the United States: prior to World War II, when imports from Eastern Europe received the same tariff treatment accorded those from any other nation, American trade with this region amounted to less than 3 percent of

Table 7-4
Commodity Composition of CEMA Foreign Trade[a] (percentage of total)

	Broad Div. I Industrial Machinery & Equipment	Broad Div. II Fuels, Raw Materials, Metals	Broad Div. III Foodstuffs & Raw Material for Foodstuffs	Broad Div. IV Industrial Consumer Goods	Not Specified
			Exports		
1950	14.2	40.9	21.8	10.6	12.4
1955	21.2	47.6	14.5	6.4	10.3
1956	22.1	47.6	12.8	7.7	9.7
1957	21.4	47.4	16.4	7.9	6.9
1958	25.4	46.0	13.8	8.7	6.0
1959	24.4	43.8	15.3	8.2	6.4
1960	26.5	45.1	14.7	8.8	4.8
1961	24.2	44.8	15.8	9.3	5.7
1962	25.0	42.5	14.9	9.0	8.4
1963	27.2	42.4	14.9	9.0	6.4
1964	28.0	44.0	12.6	8.7	6.6
1965	27.8	43.5	13.0	8.9	6.7
1966	28.1	42.3	13.4	9.3	6.8
1967	28.1	40.3	15.2	9.8	6.6
1968	28.8	39.9	13.6	10.1	7.5
1969	29.7	39.2	13.7	9.7	7.5
			Imports		
1950	23.3	54.1	14.4	5.1	3.0
1955	27.2	47.5	19.1	4.4	1.8
1956	24.4	50.7	16.3	7.2	1.4
1957	22.1	51.9	16.0	8.6	1.2
1958	23.7	49.9	14.4	10.6	1.3
1959	26.7	46.5	13.9	11.7	1.1
1960	28.8	46.1	14.0	11.0	0.9
1961	29.9	44.6	13.3	11.0	1.1
1962	34.1	41.9	11.7	11.3	0.9
1963	34.2	39.8	13.0	11.7	1.1
1964	33.4	38.8	16.4	9.9	1.4
1965	33.3	39.7	15.5	9.8	1.5
1966	34.3	39.1	14.6	10.6	1.3
1967	36.3	35.8	12.7	12.1	2.9
1968	36.4	36.0	11.9	12.5	3.1
1969	36.4	36.5	11.5	12.3	3.2

[a]excluding East Germany
Source: Based on Marer, pp. 52, 61.

all United States foreign trade.[8] This again reflects the tendency of the East Europeans to trade with their neighbors in West Europe for reasons of geographic proximity and the complementary nature of their economies.

Immediately after World War II some trading occurred, averaging approximately 2 percent of our exports and somewhat less of our imports. However, within a few years the United States as part of the Cold War policy placed severe restrictions on trade with Communist countries; and this, as Table 7-5 shows, practically wiped out all United States exports to East Europe and the Soviet Union from 1951 to 1955. The Export Control Act of 1949, with its various amendments, provided the President with broad discretionary authority to prevent or limit the export of commodities which are in short supply or whose shipment would be inconsistent with the foreign policy of the United States or impair its national security. Over the years Congress has made these controls even broader to restrict the export of items affecting the military or economic potential of the Communists.

Under the present system, most exports to East Europe require special licenses, and these licenses are not issued when the effect is considered detrimental by the federal government. The primary responsibility in this area rests with the Department of Commerce, which has attempted to employ the restrictions in such a way as to allow variations in treatment of individual countries and different political situations.

Another piece of legislation still in force is the Mutual Defense Assistance Control Act of 1951 (or the Battle Act after Congressman Laurie Battle). After passage of the Export Control Act, the United States sought and obtained multilateral cooperation from its allies in the selective control of exports to the Communist Bloc. Committees were set up to coordinate United States lists of embargoed goods with those of other countries, and the purpose of the Battle Act was to bolster this cooperation by restricting American aid to nations who export strategic items to Communist countries.

In addition to these two laws, there are many other restrictions on trade with Communist countries; two of them should be mentioned here. First, the United States has not extended most-favored-nation (MFN) treatment to imports from Communist countries with the exception of Yugoslavia and—since 1960—Poland; this implies that the imports from these countries are subject to the very high tariff rates of the Tariff Act of 1930 (The Smoot-Hawley Tariff Act). These rates are some two to four times the present rates, depending on the concessions since granted through application of the MFN principle.[9] Second, "a 1968 law prohibits the Export-Import Bank from granting or guaranteeing credit for exports destined for any communist country unless, as in the case of Romania, the President determines otherwise. But even a determination by the President does not automatically clear the way for increased credits."[10]

Returning to Table 7-5, one can observe that United States imports were affected by this legislation, although not as severely as our exports. There was a

Table 7-5
United States Trade with CEMA (millions of current dollars)ᵃ

	Bulgaria	Czechoslovakia	East Germany	Hungary	Poland	Rumania	U.S.S.R.	Total
Exports								
1946-50*	1.5	41.9	n.a.	7.2	75.8	6.0	108.6	241.0**
1951-55*	0	0.9	n.a.	0.8	1.3	0.1	0.1	3.2
1956-60*	0.2	2.3	1.2	2.4	80.0	1.1	11.3	98.5
1961	0	7.2	2.8	1.3	74.7	1.4	45.6	133.0
1962	0	7.0	1.7	0.8	74.4	0.8	20.1	125.0
1963	0.1	9.8	6.4	17.3	108.7	1.2	22.9	166.4
1964	4.8	11.3	19.9	13.6	137.9	5.1	146.4	339.0
1965	3.6	27.6	12.6	9.3	35.2	6.3	44.3	138.9
1966	3.6	37.2	24.9	10.0	52.9	27.2	41.7	197.4
1967	4.2	19.0	26.3	7.5	60.8	16.7	60.2	194.7
1968	4.0	14.1	29.2	11.0	82.2	18.2	57.4	216.1
1969	4.6	14.3	32.4	7.1	52.6	32.3	104.8	248.1
Imports								
1946-50*	3.4	22.4	n.a.	1.4	3.5	0.4	68.4	99.5*
1951-55*	0.4	6.6	n.a.	2.2	16.6	0.4	16.8	43.0*
1956-60*	0.7	9.1	4.7	1.4	31.4	0.8	21.9	70.0
1961	1.2	9.2	2.5	2.0	41.2	1.3	22.8	80.2
1962	1.2	9.9	3.0	1.7	45.6	0.6	16.4	78.4
1963	1.1	9.9	3.2	1.5	42.7	0.8	21.2	80.4
1964	1.1	12.8	6.7	1.7	54.2	1.2	21.5	99.2
1965	1.7	16.7	6.5	2.1	65.9	1.8	42.7	137.4
1966	2.5	27.7	8.2	3.5	82.9	4.7	49.6	178.6
1967	2.8	26.2	5.6	3.9	91.0	6.2	41.2	176.7
1968	3.7	23.8	5.9	3.8	96.9	5.8	58.1	198.0
1969	1.6	24.1	8.0	4.1	97.8	8.0	51.5	195.1

ᵃFigures may not add to total because of rounding.
*Annual average
**Excludes trade with East Germany
Source: Marer, tables F-1 through F-9

drop from the $99.5 million 1946-50 annual average to an average of $43 million in the next five years; but then this has been followed by almost continuous growth, although the level is still relatively and absolutely small for both sides. A study conducted for the U.S. Tariff Commission by Anton Malish analyzed the effects of this discriminatory tariff policy and found that it generally constituted less of a handicap to trade than is commonly supposed. He suggests, however, that there is evidence that the discrimination has become more burdensome to East Europe in recent years than it was when imposed due to concessions granted since then, and that this burden has been unequally distributed among CEMA, with most of it falling on countries other than the USSR. Further, it was found that this tariff policy was also largely ineffective as a means of protecting domestic production, since it is unlikely that this production would have been stimulated by a measure which affected only a minute share of United States imports.[11]

On the export side, United States controls were moderated in 1957 and again in the mid-1960s as part of President Johnson's program to build bridges between East and West. This liberalization has continued through the Nixon administration, although Congress has not yet granted the President the authority to provide any other communist countries with MFN treatment. The results of the United States policy of embargo on exports to communist nations have also been found to be rather meager.[12] Adler-Karlson estimates that allowing for Soviet countermeasures, Soviet growth during the 1950s was slowed down by six months at the most, and today it would be impossible to maintain that restrictions on East-West trade can to an appreciable degree slow down the rate of growth of the Soviet economy or the military sector of that economy.[13] He also reasons that the harm done to the other economies of East Europe must have been more serious due to the greater relative importance of trade in these countries.

In any case, whether it was because of the limited effectiveness of the embargo policy or for other reasons, such as the pursuit of profit or the pursuit of peace, the United States has been loosening its controls by allowing more and more items to be shipped to the East without a specific license, or simply by approving licenses where these continue to be necessary. The present administration during the past few years has accelerated this trend. It should be pointed out that the history of postwar American foreign economic policy toward East Europe and the Soviet Union is the history of an almost continuous conflict between the legislative and executive branches of our government, the most recent example of which is the reluctance of the United States Senate to ratify the Soviet-American Trade Agreement, which was signed in October of 1972.[14]

What is the potential for U.S.-East European (including Soviet) trade? Malish suggests that based on past experience, the level of economic activity in the United States and the development of East Europe, it is considerable: merely to regain the prewar relative economic importance of this trade to the United

States would require a volume of trade about five times that actually realized in 1970.[15] To begin our own analysis of this question, let us examine the trends in the commodity composition of our trade with this area. Table 7-6 is taken directly from Marer's extremely valuable statistical compendium.

Probably the most significant development made clear by this table is the increasing importance of manufactured goods in our trade with CEMA: in 1965 for the first time more than one-half the value of our imports from the group were manufactures, and in 1969 the composition of our exports to the area was also reversed. On both sides of the ledger, however, trade in primary goods is still quite substantial, and within that category food continues to dominate. As one can see from the table, United States imports of food have exhibited a steady growth, while our exports have fluctuated wildly reflecting the gyrations in CEMAs need for imports, which in turn reflect the cyclical performance of the agricultural sector in these economies. Next, note that although United States imports of fuels and related material have been increasing since 1966, at least through 1969 we were still a net exporter of such products to the bloc. Perhaps this situation has turned itself around since then, but in either case potential certainly exists for expanded trade. Another area where import potential seems to be growing is in the manufactured area other than chemicals and machinery.

The commodity composition of our trade, of course, varies from country to country within the group. Therefore, let us continue by very briefly describing the major aspects of our trade with each of the smaller countries of East Europe before turning to U.S.-Soviet trade which should be examined in more detail.

Bulgaria. Although there has been some recent growth in trade with Bulgaria, it is still our least important trading partner in CEMA. The United States imports principally food and live animals—especially since 1965—and some chemicals. The United States has exported mostly food, with some chemicals, machinery, and transportation equipment since 1964.

Czechoslovakia. The United States imports some food and chemicals, but almost 90 percent of the total is in the form of manufactured goods, machinery, and transportation equipment. The United States exports mainly primary goods, especially food and raw materials, although there has been some increase in manufactured products, particularly machinery and transportation equipment after 1965.

East Germany. The United States imports some raw materials, but between 85 and 90 percent of its imports are manufactured products. United States exports are more than 90 percent primary, with food alone accounting for about two-thirds of the total.

Hungary. The United States imports some food, but nearly 70 percent of this

Table 7-6
United States Trade with European CEMA: Total, 1946-1969, by SITC Categories, 1961-1969 (Millions of Current Dollars)

Year	Primary 0	1	2	3	4	Total	Manufactured 5	6	7	8	9	Total	Total Trade
						Imports (f.o.b.)							
1946-50*													99.5**
1951-55*													43.0**
1956-60*													70.0
1961	30.5	.2	16.1	.2	—	47.1	11.0	11.4	3.2	7.4	.4	33.2	80.2
1962	28.3	.2	18.5	.2	—	47.3	5.1	13.4	3.6	8.5	.8	30.8	78.4
1963	26.7	.3	20.6	.3	—	47.9	2.9	17.1	3.1	8.6	.5	32.4	80.4
1964	30.1	.3	22.6	.5	0	53.5	2.5	28.0	3.9	10.7	.6	45.8	99.2
1965	38.6	.3	21.6	.6	0	61.3	3.8	52.2	5.6	13.4	.9	76.2	137.4
1966	47.4	.5	26.1	.6	0	74.6	9.5	63.8	13.6	15.8	.9	103.4	178.6
1967	54.2	.6	21.1	1.1	2.0	79.0	7.7	56.2	13.5	19.1	1.2	97.7	176.7
1968	52.2	.7	23.3	1.5	0	78.1	8.3	80.9	9.1	20.2	1.3	120.1	198.0
1969	55.5	.8	22.5	4.4	0	83.3	7.4	71.4	9.4	22.4	1.1	111.8	195.1
						Exports (f.o.b.)							
1946-50*													241.0**
1951-55*													3.2**
1956-60*													98.5
1961	37.6	1.1	32.4	.4	24.7	96.3	6.1	6.8	20.5	1.3	1.9	36.8	133.0
1962	50.7	1.4	38.1	.1	15.8	106.2	4.0	2.1	7.6	1.5	3.4	18.4	125.0
1963	97.5	4.0	30.4	3.6	7.7	143.2	11.0	2.1	4.5	1.2	4.2	23.2	166.4
1964	225.3	4.2	46.1	4.5	30.4	310.4	12.5	2.4	7.5	1.7	4.4	28.4	339.0
1965	40.5	2.3	38.5	2.5	28.7	112.7	9.5	2.6	10.7	2.2	1.3	26.3	138.9
1966	75.7	3.4	57.9	2.5	13.5	153.0	10.2	5.3	24.6	3.6	.7	44.4	197.4
1967	60.2	3.9	58.4	1.3	4.1	127.9	22.7	8.1	30.6	4.1	1.0	66.5	194.7
1968	78.6	3.7	53.1	2.2	4.2	141.9	25.6	7.1	33.0	7.7	.6	74.2	216.1
1969	48.9	4.0	54.2	6.0	1.4	114.8	35.0	23.5	65.5	7.8	1.2	133.1	248.1

*Annual average.

**Excludes trade with East Germany.

Standard International Trade Classification (SITC) Categories:
0 Food and Live Animals
1 Beverages and Tobacco
2 Crude Materials, Inedible, Except Fuels
3 Mineral Fuels, Lubricants and Related Materials
4 Animal and Vegetable Oils and Fats
5 Chemicals
6 Manufactured Goods classified chiefly by Material
7 Machinery and Transport Equipment
8 Miscellaneous Manufactured Articles
9 Commodities and Transactions, not classified according to kind

Source:
Paul Marer, *Soviet and East European Foreign Trade, 1946-1969*, table F-9. © 1972 by Indiana University Press, Bloomington. Reprinted by permission of the publisher. SITC categories are listed by Marer on p. 7.

relatively underdeveloped country's sales to the United States are manufactures. The United States exports mostly food and some raw materials and chemicals.

Poland. Poland has traditionally been our largest trading partner in East Europe. Only in the last two or three years has the USSR moved ahead of Poland in this respect. United States imports are mostly primary goods, especially foods which account for about 50 percent of the total. However, the share of manufactured goods has grown rapidly since 1964. United States exports are almost entirely in the primary area, more or less evenly divided between food and raw materials.

Rumania. Trade with this country has grown quite rapidly in the last six or seven years. United States imports have usually been dominated by manufactured products, but in this recent growth fuels and lubricants have played an important role, one which could become more important now that our tariffs and quotas on these have been removed. United States exports were mostly primary goods when trade was small, but are now manufactured (more than one-half) as well as raw material.

Finally, let us turn to our trade with the Soviet Union. To put the current picture in perspective it would be useful to examine at least briefly the trade between these two countries in the period prior to World War II, and this has been done in Table 7-7, where data are available from 1910 through 1942. It can be seen that the volume of United States *exports* to the Soviet Union has fluctuated fantastically in this period, with the heaviest activity being during the war years of 1915, 1916, 1917, and 1942. Relatively speaking however, imports from the United States were also important to the Soviet economy during a large number of years in the 1920s and 1930s, when the United States was one of the USSR's major trading partners along with Great Britain and Germany.[16] Throughout the prewar period the relative significance of U.S.-USSR trade was much greater to the Soviet Union (even on the export side, but especially on the import side) than to the United States. Imports from the Soviet Union for example never exceeded 2 percent of all United States imports, and other than the four war years already mentioned, exports to the Soviets did not constitute more than 5 percent of the U.S. total.

In the period after World War II, as Table 7-8 demonstrates, the relative importance of trade for both countries fell sharply from the prewar pattern. Immediately after the war, there was a substantial amount of trade as part of the postwar recovery effort. However, at the beginning of the 1950s Congress enacted the legislation referred to earlier and effectively shut off all but an average of $100,000 of exports to the USSR and forced our imports back to little more than one-half the level of the 1930s. Again, there was some relaxation on the part of the United States during the second half of the 1950s, and this is reflected especially in the export statistics. Notice, however, that the trade between these two nations began to grow in the last years of the 1960s, and this illustrates the increasing willingness of each government to increase commercial relations with the other. For the Soviets, it is a part of their movement away

Table 7-7
United States-Soviet Trade: 1910-42

	Volume of Trade (millions of current dollars)		Percentage of U.S. Total Trade		Percentage of USSR Total Trade	
	Exports	Imports	Exports	Imports	Exports	Imports
1910-14 ave.	24.6	20.9	1.1	1.2	n.a.	n.a.
1915	170.0	3.1	4.8	0.2	n.a.	n.a.
1916	470.5	8.6	8.6	0.4	n.a.	n.a.
1917	424.5	14.5	6.8	0.5	n.a.	n.a.
1918	17.3	10.8	0.3	0.4	9.4	13.6
1919	83.4	9.7	1.0	0.2	*	*
1920	28.7	12.5	0.3	0.2	*	*
1921	15.6	1.3	0.3	0.1	*	19.2
1922	29.9	1.0	0.8	*	*	16.2
1923	7.6	1.6	0.2	*	0.4	3.0
1924	42.1	8.2	0.9	0.2	1.9	21.8
1925	68.9	13.1	1.4	0.3	4.9	27.9
1926	49.9	14.1	1.0	0.3	4.4	16.2
1927	64.9	12.9	1.3	0.3	2.9	20.4
1928	74.1	14.0	1.4	0.3	3.5	19.8
1929	84.0	22.5	1.6	0.5	4.6	20.2
1930	14.4	24.4	3.0	0.8	3.9	25.0
1931	103.7	13.2	4.3	0.6	2.8	20.8
1932	12.6	9.7	0.8	0.7	3.0	4.5
1933	9.0	12.1	0.5	0.8	2.8	4.8
1934	15.0	12.3	0.7	0.7	3.4	7.7
1935	24.7	17.8	1.1	0.9	7.2	12.2
1936	33.4	20.5	1.4	0.8	9.6	15.4
1937	42.9	30.8	1.3	1.1	7.7	18.3
1938	69.7	24.0	2.3	1.2	6.6	28.3
1939	56.6	25.0	1.8	1.1	14.0	30.7
1940	86.9	22.3	2.2	0.8	8.0	31.0
1941	108.0	30.0	2.1	0.9	n.a.	n.a.
1942	1,379.0	25.0	17.6	0.9	n.a.	n.a.

*Less than 0.1%

Sources:

Mikhail V. Condoide, *Russian-American Trade*, (Columbus, Ohio: Bureau of Business Research, Ohio State University, 1946), p. 91: all but USSR percentages.

Ministerstvo Vneshnei Torgovli SSSR, *Vneshnaia torgovlia SSSR: 1918-1966*, (Moscow: Mezhdunarodnye Otnosheniia, 1967), pp. 8-13: USSR percentages.

Table 7-8
United States-Soviet Trade: 1946-72

	Volume of Trade (millions of current dollars)		Percentage of U.S. Total Trade		Percentage of USSR Total Trade	
	(1) Exports	(2) Imports	(3) Exports	(4) Imports	(5) Exports	(6) Imports
1946-50 ave.	108.6	68.4	0.1	1.0	5.7	9.5
1951-55 ave.	0.1	16.8	*	0.1	0.5	*
1956-60 ave.	11.3	21.9	0.1	0.2	0.4	0.2
1961	45.6	22.8	0.2	0.2	0.4	0.8
1962	20.1	16.4	0.1	0.1	0.2	0.3
1963	22.9	21.2	0.1	0.1	0.3	0.3
1964	146.4	21.5	0.6	0.1	0.3	1.9
1965	44.3	42.7	0.2	0.2	0.5	0.5
1966	41.7	49.6	0.1	0.2	0.6	0.5
1967	60.2	41.2	0.2	0.2	0.4	0.7
1968	57.4	58.1	0.2	0.2	0.5	0.6
1969	104.8	51.5	0.3	0.1	0.4	1.0
1970	118.4	72.2	0.3	0.2	0.6	1.0
1971	160.6	56.8	0.4	0.1	0.7	1.3
1972	550.3	95.8	1.3	0.2	n.a.	n.a.

*Less than 0.1%.

Sources:

Marer, p. 62 and table F-1: cols. (1), (2), (5), and (6), 1946-69. U.S. Department of Commerce, *Survey of Current Business*, February, 1973, pp. s-21, s-22: cols. (1)-(4), 1970-72, February 1965-1970, pp. s-21, s-22, used for cols. (3)-(4), 1964-69. U.S. Bureau of the Census, *Foreign Commerce and Navigation of the United States, 1946-1963* (Washington: U.S. Government Printing Office, 1965), pp. 1-2: cols. (3)-(4), 1946-63.

International Development Research Center, "Soviet and East European Trade Data Bank: 1970-71" used for cols. (5)-(6), 1970-71.

from the policy of autarky and also indicates an increasing appreciation of the principle of comparative advantage. For the United States, I would say it has been a function of several variables, first and foremost a change in the United States attitude concerning trade with communist countries: it still seems strange, but the hope is that it will make for a more peaceful coexistence; second, an appreciation of the relatively minor effect our earlier policies have had, particularly when compared with their costs; third, an increasing reluctance by American business to continue to forgo business opportunities where others are already substantially involved. There are other factors which we discuss later on, but these are the major ones, in my opinion.

It should be pointed out that even in the most recent years the relative significance of U.S.-USSR trade has not even approached its prewar level. For example, 1972 was a record year for United States exports to the USSR, but they only amounted to a little over one percent of our exports. On the Soviet side, 1972 did find the United States once again among the top five trading partners of the USSR. More than half of United States exports to the USSR that year were grains, but there was also a significant amount of trade in other products such as chemicals, machinery, and equipment. There were large Soviet purchases, for instance, of pipeline laying machinery from the International Harvester Company and the Caterpillar Tractor Company, as well as foundry equipment for the Kama River truck project.[17] The latter is particularly important because it signifies an acceleration in the trend begun in the mid-1960s toward a greater willingness to trade with the Soviet Union: in the last quarter of 1971, licenses for $1 billion worth of equipment were approved for the Kama River plant, which contrasts with the situation the previous year when Mack as well as Ford, each admittedly having its own doubts about bidding for the project, were strongly warned off from doing so by influential authorities in Washington.[18]

Since one often hears the objection to increased trade because of limited possibilities for Soviet exports to the United States, it is worthy to note that United States imports from the USSR in 1972 also took a very sizable jump, especially in the last six months, during which their average level rose by 40 percent over that of the first half of the year. The surprising thing is that, contrary to what might be expected, about two-thirds of our imports from the Soviet Union have been manufactured products, and this is just about the same as their share in our aggregate imports.[19] I think we can say, therefore, on the basis of the recent trends, that we have seen significant growth in United States trade with East Europe and especially the Soviet Union. The question is: will this growth continue? I would now like to address myself to this topic.

Problems and Prospects

First, there is a set of problems facing the East European countries, problems which generally are not in the area of foreign trade, but which do have implications for it. Probably the most obvious are the internal economic difficulties which most of these countries have experienced in the last decade, and which have resulted in considerable debate and reform in the group. Perhaps the major problem has been that of pricing, which has been of limited value in the process of rational economic decision-making. In part this has been due to Marxist ideology, and in part the gigantic difficulty of replacing the market by an administrative hierarchy. The absence of an internal pricing system which properly reflects scarcity implies that the conduct of foreign trade will tend to be irrational if based on internal prices. The CEMA countries have attempted to circumvent this problem by employing world market prices as the starting point for their foreign trade negotiations even among themselves, and:

according to the most recent authoritative document on the future of CEMA cooperation (Complex Program-1971), during the next 6 to 8 years, intra-CEMA prices will continue to be based on world market prices of a previous period and will remain fixed for several years.[20]

Clearly, this is a second best solution to the problem, since world prices are not likely to coincide with the true opportunity costs in these individual economies. This means that even if East Europe is no longer committed to autarky, it will be difficult for it to exploit its comparative advantage to the fullest extent if the advantage cannot accurately be measured.

Two developments have led to some improvement, however. First is the economic reform which has introduced capital charges, land rents, and some degree of price responsiveness to market forces in almost all of the countries (the major exception being the Soviet Union).[21] Secondly, the reforms have attempted to make it possible for foreign trade to serve as a competitive stimulus by permitting more direct connections between domestic producers and foreign markets and by introducing some flexibility into the foreign trade sector, which has traditionally been one of the most tightly controlled in the Soviet type economy.[22]

Another alleged cause of the slowdown in the economic growth of most of these economies in the late 1950s and early 1960s was the so-called incentive problem: labor productivity increases had slowed, and one of the reasons given was that workers were not sufficiently motivated by the rewards they received. Their money incomes were definitely rising, but at a much faster rate than the availability of the kinds of consumer goods on which they wanted to spend their money.[23] Exporting surplus consumer items and importing deficit ones is therefore seen as part of the solution to this problem.

A problem related to that of growth is that some of the CEMA countries, such as the USSR, may not be able to exploit their resources at what they consider a satisfactory pace. So they turn to others like the U.S. or Japan for assistance. Japan already has begun cooperating in the development of the Soviet Far East, and United States companies have been talking about multibillion dollar investments to tap Soviet resources.[24]

Another issue of interest here is the economic integration of East Europe. Although CEMA has had some achievements, it has not been particularly successful in bringing about a true economic integration of the Soviet Union and East Europe, primarily because of the nationalistic tendencies of the individual countries outside of the USSR. However, in the last five years or so, there does seem to be some attempt to promote integration within the limits set by the individual nations. For instance, a bank has been formed for assisting in the balancing of trade accounts, another has been formed to help finance long term investment projects, and a number of joint projects among CEMA members have been undertaken. At least one East European economist has suggested that this trend will continue and will "create new impulses for the development of trade with Western countries."[25] The reasons he gave included: (1) integration will stimulate new growth which will stimulate import demand; (2) these countries are no longer aiming at even some sort of bloc autarky; and (3) integration will accelerate modernization and specialization, which will in turn lower production costs and improve the quality of products, which in turn will increase the competitiveness of their products on world markets. The problem of product quality has been one of the major stumbling blocks to East-West trade in the past, so that anything that can alleviate it will tend to raise the potential for trade.

Another set of problems which impinge more directly on trade include the following. The fact that the ruble is employed in bloc trading, and that the bloc currencies are not freely convertible, has increased the difficulties of international trade. The trade within CEMA itself has been hampered by this element, and there is continuing discussion of the possibility of convertibility. Bilateral trade arrangements have been a hallmark of East European trade, and this tends to restrict the volume of trade that actually takes place, since the aim is to balance each nation's trade with each of its trading partners. An increased willingness to employ multilateral arrangements seems to be emerging, and this would tend to increase the overall potential for trade and be especially important for U.S.-Soviet trade, which traditionally has shown an imbalance in favor of the United States. As Gregory Grossman has recently pointed out, if this historical pattern continues:

the USSR will have to generate a growing positive balance in its trade with the rest of the hard-currency area in order to finance its growing purchases here and to repay the credits that may be extended in the meantime. In this sense, the future of US-Soviet trade is intimately related to the future of Soviet trade with Western Europe and Japan. With time, the latter may turn out to be of particular importance. The enormous trade potential across the Sea of Japan may harbor one of the main keys for the long-term expansion of US-Soviet trade.[26]

Quality is one factor involved in selling to the hard currency area. Action is being taken on this through the reforms and the integration mentioned above, but Western businessmen are also helping. Barter and switch-trading houses, which specialize in deals with primitive forms of payment, are playing a role, but so are manufacturing companies themselves—by engaging in either straight barter or more complicated arrangements such as counter-purchase (arranging to sell Russian products in the West in return for selling their product to the Russians) or product—payback (where the Russians might be sold a factory and use the output of the factory to pay for it).[27]

With respect to our trade with CEMA, a factor to consider is how well American companies and the state enterprises of these countries work together in joint venture agreements. Since the Soviet enterprises in particular have been isolated from the outside for more than fifty years, it can be argued that they will have difficulties operating in the Western environment and hence will need to set up joint ventures in which American firms could contribute their marketing as well as technological skills.[28] Can individuals coming from societies with competing economic systems and political philosophies work closely in harmony? At first glance, the prospects might seem doubtful; nevertheless, progress is being made in working out difficulties as they occur—the increased trade already shows this—and both sides are gaining experience all this time.

Another variable which should be examined as to its influence on future trade is American government policy. To the extent that there is concern for our balances of payments deficits, one would expect that East-West trade would be encouraged, since it has traditionally been true that the United States exports exceed United States imports from Eastern Europe. (See Table 7-6.) Secondly, and perhaps more importantly, our total foreign policy toward this area of the world has been more amicable of late: some examples include the SALT talks, talks on force reduction, talks on Vietnam, President Nixon's visit to Moscow, and Brezhnev's visit to the United States. A more open approach to trade would certainly fit into this pattern, and I think we have begun to see it. The list of controlled items for which a specific license is required has been cut,[29] and where licenses are still required, they have been obtained more easily than previously. The most recent step toward freer trade between the United States and the Soviet Union was the Soviet-American Trade Agreement signed in October 1972. Probably the most important point of the treaty is that it would give MFN treatment to the Soviet Union, but it also contained other important articles. One provided that each government would encourage and facilitate trade (which means we would try to obtain credits which the Soviets would need in many cases), and it envisioned at least a tripling of total bilateral trade compared with the 1969-71 period over the three years covered by the agreement.[30] This would require at least a matching of 1972's record level of business.

Unfortunately, the Senate has not yet approved this agreement. Senator Jackson formulated an amendment which would deny most-favored-nation treatment to the Soviet Union unless the Soviets removed all restrictions on emigration, but since that Mr. Brezhnev provided assurances that the so-called education tax had been suspended. The administration's omnibus trade bill includes MFN treatment for other Communist countries as well, but as of January 1974, the bill still had not been approved by both houses or Congress.

In conclusion, I would say that there seem to be a great many obstacles in the path of a large and rapid expansion in United States trade with the Soviet Union and East Europe, but that in almost every case there are forces in operation to reduce the size of these obstacles. The long run potential for trade appears to be quite substantial if these forces continue to operate.

Notes

1. For a systematic comparison of the reforms in the individual countries see: Frederic L. Pryor, "Barriers to Market Socialism in Eastern Europe in the Mid 1960s," *Studies in Comparative Communism*, vol. 3, April 1970, pp. 31-64.

2. The average annual growth of exports for the world (including the CEMA nations) from 1952-71 was 8.0 percent, according to data available in the United Nations, *Yearbook of International Trade Statistics 1970-71* (New York: United Nations, 1973), Table A.

3. Stefan C. Stolte, "East-West Trade in the Seventies," *Bulletin of the Institute for the Study of the USSR*, vol. 17, September 1970, p. 17.

4. A more detailed description of the history of Soviet foreign trade may be found in Leon M. Herman, *Studies on the Soviet Union*, vol. 7, pp. 67-102, no. 1, 1967, also reprinted in Morris Bornstein and Daniel R. Fusfeld, *The Soviet Economy* (Homewood, Ill.: Irwin, 1970), pp. 260-288.

5. Paul Marer, *Soviet and East European Foreign Trade, 1946-1969: A Statistical Compendium and Guide* (Bloomington: University of Indiana Press, 1972), p. 43.

6. Nicolas Spulber, *The Economics of Communist Eastern Europe* (New York: M.I.T. & Wiley, 1957), p. 410.

7. Ibid., p. 415.

8. Anton F. Malish Jr., *United States East European Trade*, Staff Research Studies, no. 4 (Washington: U.S. Tariff Commission, 1972), p. 2.

9. Ibid., p. 10.

10. Peter G. Peterson, *US-Soviet Commercial Relationships in a New Era* (Washington: U.S. Department of Commerce, August 1972), p. 18.

11. Malish, op. cit., pp. 13-17.

12. J. Wilczynski, "The Strategic Embargo in Perspective," *Soviet Studies*, vol. 19, July 1967, pp. 74-86; and Gunnar Adler-Karlson, *Western Economic Warfare: 1947-1967* (Stockholm: Almqvist and Wiksell, 1968).

13. Adler-Karlson, op. cit., pp. 5-8.

14. This conflict is described and discussed in detail in a recent study by David W. Folts, "The Role of the President and Congress in Formulation of the United States Economic Policy Toward the SovietUnion, 1947-1968," (Ph.D. dissertation, University of Notre Dame, 1970).

15. Malish, op. cit., p. 4.

16. Ministerstvo Vneshnei Torgovli SSSR, *Vneshniaia torgovlia SSSR: 1918-1966* (Moscow: Mezhdunarodnye Otnoshenlia, 1967), pp. 8-14.

17. *New York Times*, February 9, 1973, pp. 45, 51.

18. "A Scent of Honey: A Survey of East-West Trade," *The Economist*, vol. 246, January 6, 1973, survey p. 10.

19. Marer, table F-1.

20. Paul Marer, *Postwar Pricing and Price Patterns in Socialist Foreign Trade (1946-1971)*, IDRC Report 1, (Bloomington: University of Indiana, 1972), p. 7.

21. Pryor, op. cit., pp. 50-55.

22. Ibid., pp. 47-48.

23. This particular problem is discussed more fully in R. Skurski, "The Buyers' Market and Soviet Consumer Goods Distribution," *Slavic Review*, vol. 31, December 1972, pp. 817-830.

24. *The Wall Street Journal*, April 10, 1973, p. 40.

25. Zbigniew Kamecki, "Possibilities of Increasing East-West Trade and Industrial Cooperation," *Soviet and East European Foreign Trade*, vol. 9, Spring 1973, p. 82.

26. Gregory Grossman, "US-Soviet Trade and Economic Relations: Problems and Prospects," *Association for Comparative Economic Studies Bulletin*, vol. 15, Spring 1973, p. 22.

27. *The Economist* vol. 246, op. cit., survey pp. 16-17.

28. *The Wall Street Journal*, March 29, 1973, p. 14.

29. Ibid.

30. "Soviet-American Trade Agreement," *The American Review of East-West Trade*, vol. 5, November 1972, p. 19.

8

The People's Republic of China: The Market of the Future?

Robert F. Dernberger
University of Michigan

China's Foreign Trade Heritage

About one hundred and fifty years ago, few Western merchant traders knew much about or had any interest in the China market. For centuries, China had been isolated from the West, and the early attempts of first the Arabs, then the Portuguese, and then the Dutch to establish trade ties with the Chinese did not lead to any significant or continuous trade. With the emergence of England as a major trading power and her establishment of a significant colonial empire on the continent of Southeast Asia, attempts to create trade ties with the Chinese met with greater success. The British success, however, was due to their willingness to reach a workable compromise with the Chinese attitude of superiority, their restriction of the resulting trade, and the benefits the trade yielded to the Chinese. English trade with China was regulated within the institution of a bilateral monopoly, the East Indian Company having monopoly control over the Western traders and a merchant guild of thirteen Chinese merchants representing the Chinese, with the trade itself limited to the port of Canton on the Southeast coast of China. The fundamental basis of the trade was the triangular trade between England, India, and China: the ships of the East India Company carrying British textiles to India, silver to China, and Chinese tea and silk back to England.

To a mercantilist, of course, this loss of silver was a dead weight loss to England and a gain to China. What was needed was a commodity with a high value per unit of weight produced in India and which was in demand in China. Such a commodity was found in opium and by the 1830s, China was importing opium in exchange for exports of tea and silk, a trade viewed by the Chinese government as a dead weight loss. At the same time, however, the institutional framework for China's foreign trade was also breaking down, the East India Company having lost its monopoly of the trade in 1832. Private merchants, never happy with the need to act as agents of the East India Company, had been successful in their attempts to remove the Company's monopoly, not on the basis of their own appeals to Parliament, for they lacked the political power to achieve that result, but by their ability to create the myth of a huge China market in the eyes of the Manchester textile producers who did have the necessary political power.

The vision of 400 million Chinese wearing textiles woven in England was a very powerful argument, and it was easy for the private merchants to blame their lack of success on the monopoly of the East India Company. Once the monopoly on the Western side of the trade was removed, however, the private merchants merely ran up against the intransigent monopoly of Chinese merchants. On the other hand, when the Chinese decided to stop the trade in opium by seizing and burning the supplies of the drug in Canton, they were no longer dealing with the East India Company, but with the Superintendent of Trade, an agent of the British Crown who could call upon British gunboats to open China to the Western trader. The results of the ensuing gunboat diplomacy were to be expected: successive Chinese military defeats and treaties which opened up additional areas of China to the penetration of foreign trade and investment. Yet, the visions of a huge Chinese market were soon dispelled, and it was not until the turn of the century that the Chinese market was penetrated by a foreign product: kerosene for the lamps of China.

Before the turn of the century, however, many enterprising Western merchants were lured to China in the hopes of gaining access to its huge consumer market. One such dreamer was the merchant who, not realizing that the Chinese suffered a very low per capita income but enjoyed a rich cultural heritage of music not based on the octave scale, believed it should be easy to sell a piano to just one out of every 1,000 Chinese families or a sale of 80,000 pianos. He ended up with a warehouse full of pianos in Hong Kong which he had to sell at a loss.

We now possess a much better knowledge of China and most United States businessmen have adopted both a more cautious and a more well-informed approach to potential trade with China. Nonetheless, the population of China has increased to over 750 million and, with the recent rapid and significant relaxation of controls on trade with China, we can easily find a modern counterpart to our piano salesman of a century ago. For example, there is the Chicago cosmetic firm which sought my services as a consultant, hoping to increase their foreign sales by entering the newly opened markets in China. Despite my attempts to throw cold water on their plans, they thanked me for my services and sent my wife a case of their products as payment, but refused to believe that the female half of 800 million people did not offer them a tremendous opportunity to increase their overseas sales. "After all, even a vigorous supporter of Mao must want to look pretty and catch a husband." Another would-be, enterprising, modern-day merchant somehow acquired a visa to attend the Canton Trade Fair, packed his bags and rushed off to capture his share of the huge China market as a representative of a large number of American producers of consumer's goods. Upon arriving in Canton, of course, he discovered the Fair was an export fair where the Chinese sell export commodities; import purchases are made according to plan by agents of the state in separate negotiations usually initiated by the Chinese. Not wanting to return home empty-handed, he purchased a large consignment of Shanghai Double Happiness ping-pong balls and paddles which are now held in a warehouse in New York to be sold at a loss because of their poor quality compared to the available supplies on the American market.

Despite these interesting anecdotes about the myth of a huge China market, the China market that does exist cannot be overlooked. While direct trade between the largest economy in the world, in terms of total output of goods and services, and the largest economy in the world, in terms of population, was not possible for two decades due to legal prohibitions, trade between those two countries is now possible, and the Chinese have shown they are willing to trade. Furthermore, there is a basic argument suggesting that the potential exists for a substantial United States trade with China. As an underdeveloped country which has launched a significant economic development program, China must rely on imports of producers goods, and the United States is the world's largest supplier of those goods.

Although the United States has now willingly relinquished to the Soviet Union its role as the major threat to China's security, a great many unresolved issues remain to be settled before relations between the United States and China can be said to be friendly. Nonetheless, if the history of China's trade relations in the past decade is any indication of China's future attitude, political differences are not a major obstacle to securing a significant share of China's foreign trade. Japan, China's traditional rival in the Far East, with a conservative government and capitalist economy, has—up until the change in United States policy—refused to extend *de jure* recognition to China; yet Japan is China's major trading partner by a wide margin. West Germany, the capitalist half of a divided country, has been China's major trading partner in Europe. Finally, Hong Kong, a colonial legacy from the age of imperialism, holds a lease on about 100 square miles of Chinese territory and has dealt forcibly with Communist-initiated labor unrest and riots; but Hong Kong is China's second largest trading partner as well as the beneficiary of large direct Chinese foreign investment. Thus, the potential for a large trade between the United States and China would appear to exist. There are, however, a great many factors which will serve to limit that potential trade.

Factors Limiting Trade

First, the basic economics of the trade itself will limit trade between the United States and China. Professor Simon Kuznets, in his massive study of the quantitative data available for the process of economic development,[1] finds that a country's participation in foreign trade is inversely related to its size, i.e., variety and quantity of resources available, level of development, and distance from the major trade routes in the Atlantic Ocean and the Mediterranean and North Seas. China, of course, has a high score on all these variables, and its low foreign trade participation rate—exports accounting for less than 5 percent of Gross Domestic Product at the prewar peak level of China foreign trade in 1928 and the same low rates during the 1950s and 1960s under the Communists[2]—is one of the lowest such rates in the world, exactly what is predicted by Kuznets' analysis.

The structure of China's foreign trade will also inhibit trade with the United States. Whereas China's demand for imports and the United States' supply of exports are complementary, China's export supply and the United States' import demand are not. This is nothing more than the traditional problem of any underdeveloped country in need of capital goods. With the major exception of those countries blessed with oil reserves, world trade is dominated by the industrial rich, and a large share of world trade consists of the bilateral exchange of industrial products between industrial countries. The industrial countries have become so specialized in production and trade that a significant share of these bilateral exchanges is within the same commodity classification in the trade statistics. The underdeveloped countries, almost by definition, export raw and processed agricultural products and are forced to engage in severe competition in the limited markets of the industrial countries or receive foreign aid to finance their producer's goods imports. China is no exception; in the 1920s two-thirds of China's exports consisted of raw and processed agricultural products (including textiles), and the only major development brought about by the changes in the structure of China's economy during the last two decades was to increase the share of processed agricultural products while the share of raw agricultural products declined, with raw and processed agricultural products together still accounting for two-thirds of China's total exports. (See Table 8-4, p. 125.)

China's imports of producer's goods are severely limited by the country's capacity to earn foreign exchange from its export trade. Not a producer of precious metals, and having inherited an empty treasury when it won the Civil War, the Chinese have been able to build up their foreign exchange holdings through remittances from Overseas Chinese, purchases of and seizures of foreign exchange held by Chinese citizens at the end of the Civil War, returns on investments abroad (especially in Hong Kong), and export surpluses. These reserves are estimated as approximately equal to three or four months worth of imports.[3] This very tight foreign exchange position is somewhat alleviated by complete state control of foreign trade transactions and nonconvertibility of the domestic currency, but it has led to a very cautious and conservative attitude concerning financing imports on long-term credits. The Chinese, of course, often insist on normal short-term credit and have earned an excellent credit rating abroad. At the present time, however, there is no indication that they are seeking long-term loans and, therefore, China's import trade will continue to be limited by the available supply of and foreign demand for China's exports.

To help solve this problem of scarce foreign exchange, China enjoys the unique position of having a sizable population living abroad, most of which is congregated in Southeast Asia, especially Hong Kong and Singapore. Not only do these Overseas Chinese remit foreign exchange to their families at home, they also buy foodstuffs, textiles, and manufactured goods exported by China. In a statistical analysis of China's market shares in the import markets of Southeast Asia—an analysis examining the explanatory power of various economic, political, and social variables—I found a very positive and significant relationship between China's market share in the imports of any particular Southeast Asian country and the share of Chinese in that country's population.[4] In commodity trade with Singapore and Hong Kong in 1971, China earned enough foreign exchange to pay for the import surpluses in its trade with Western Europe, North America, and Japan.[5] Nonetheless, unless there is an unexpected change in China's attitude as to the desirability of securing long-term loans, the limits of China's export capacity due to the low level margin of surplus and slow growth of output in the agricultural sector, the soft markets for its exports in the industrial countries, and the competition China faces in these markets will serve as a significant constraint on China's import capacity. In addition to these economic considerations, domestic institutional and basic policy factors also will serve as constraints on China's import capacity. China's foreign trade is carried out by the state trading organization, with exports determined as a residual category in domestic production and supply plans and imports dictated by those same plans.[6] On the margin, efforts are made to increase exports to raise foreign exchange earnings, while imports are reduced to conserve foreign exchange reserves and promote domestic sources of supply. In reading the reports, speeches, and analyses published by the Chinese, an underlying theme emerges: foreign trade is a necessary evil. I have come across many arguments supporting an increase in the share of domestic output going to exports, but only because of the need to finance vital imports of producers goods, not to take advantage of the gains from trade on the basis of comparisons of real costs in China and abroad. I have never encountered any discussions or come across any empirical evidence of the Chinese determining to import or export a particular commodity because the "price was right" or because a particular exchange of commodities was a savings in terms of domestic resources.

This attitude toward foreign trade and its benefits, i.e., that it serves as the means to provide producers goods necessary to achieve domestic production and investment targets, is reinforced by their basic policy of autarkic economic development. One should not uncritically label their development policy as autarkic, however. I have already argued that their foreign trade participation rate is about normal for a country with China's resource endowment, level of employment, and location. Furthermore, the Chinese themselves use the term "self-dependency" and explicitly refer to the United States as their model; they desire to be able to produce their own needs in an emergency, but will engage in normal foreign trade where their supplies and needs match other countries' needs and supplies. Quite simply, they desire to pursue the development of their infant industries as rapidly as possible so as to reduce their dependence on foreign supplies of producers goods. At the same time, however, they admit the need, despite Mao's statements urging the Chinese to rely on their own efforts, to rely on foreign producers goods and technology in the short run. Given the present level of economic development and production capabilities in China, the short run can be interpreted as the foreseeable future. Nonetheless, their basic attitude toward foreign trade and dependence on foreigners can be expected to have a limiting effect on potential trade with the United States.

A final factor limiting future trade between the United States and China has to do with inherited attitudes and policies in the United States. Despite the recent thaw in relations between the two countries, it will take some time for the iceberg to melt. The outright prohibition on exports to China has been removed, but trade with China is still subject to stringent licensing procedures. In February 1972, the Commerce Department published a list of commodities that could be exported to China under the open general export license provided by the Export Control Regulations, an action which granted China treatment similar to that granted to Russia and most other East European countries. This still leaves in effect considerable restrictions on United States trade with China, however; commodities not on the approved list for a general export license can only be exported upon receipt of a license from the Office of Export Control, U.S. Department of Commerce. Exports of "strategic" commodities, i.e., those which embody United States technology not available elsewhere, must be approved on an individual basis with the final authority for permission resting with the National Security Council. The Chinese, of course, are most interested in commodities embodying United States technology. The debate over allowing Boeing to export airplanes to China could not be resolved by the National Security Council, but went to the President for a final decision. Permission has been granted to the United States importers to import Chinese commodities into the United States, but these imports are subject to a much higher tariff than similar ones coming from countries enjoying Most Favored Nation treatment.

This list of economic and political factors involved in estimating potential trade between the United States and China leads to a rather pessimistic conclusion. Yet, inasmuch as the United States is the largest world trader and China is the seventh largest economy in the world, even a relatively small foreign trade participation rate for China would be consistent with a substantial absolute level of trade between these two countries. But how large is that trade likely to be? In 1971, I published a detailed analysis of the prospects for trade between China and the United States, with estimates for Sino-American trade in 1980.[7] Fortunately, events in the last two years have not proven me wrong, and those estimates still appear reasonable. It is not the estimates themselves, however, which are important, it is the assumptions one makes in obtaining them.

Total Chinese Trade Potential

First, one must assume that developments in China's foreign trade during the past two decades are a good guide to developments in the future. Inasmuch as exports are the residual category of domestic output and supply requirements, and imports are a derived demand from domestic production and investment activities, China's foreign trade has been a direct reflection of developments in the domestic economy. Starting from a level of 70Q million U.S. dollars in 1950, China's exports grew rapidly along with domestic production, to a level of $1.7 billion in 1956; leveled off with retrenchment in the domestic economy in 1957; jumped to a peak of $2.25 billion in 1959 as a result of the Great Leap; declined to a level of $1.5 billion in 1961-63, reflecting the domestic agricultural crisis following the failure of the Great Leap; slowly regained the peak level of $2.2 billion in 1966 with the rehabilitation of the domestic economy; suffered a dip to $2 billion in 1967-68 due to the Cultural Revolution; and increased to an all-time peak in 1971, reflecting the three very good agricultural years in 1969-71. (See Table 8-1, p. 123.) Changes in the level of imports followed a similar pattern, China incurring an import surplus while a net recipient of Soviet loans in 1950-54 and an export surplus while repaying these loans in 1956-65. Since 1965, China's foreign trade has been approximately balanced, usually showing an export surplus amounting, on the average, to 4 percent of total exports. This stable relationship between the level of trade and domestic economic activity and the pattern of a roughly balanced merchandise trade, in the absence of large-scale borrowing from abroad, is but the first step in estimating China's potential trade in the future.

Second, to use the first assumption to obtain the desired estimate we must determine what the growth rate in the Chinese economy will be and whether or not new policies will be adopted to destroy the validity of the relationship between foreign trade and domestic economic activity observed in the past. In another study currently in progress, I have developed an econometric model which specifies the relationship between seventeen different sectors, including the foreign trade sector, in China's economy.[8] I used this model to estimate China's future economic growth in my earlier paper on potential Sino-American trade. The particular policy matrix assumed in making those estimates was a continuation of the present successful policies of economic moderation fostered by the compromise leadership which has emerged following the Cultural Revolution, a leadership explicitly rejecting the radical and unsuccessful programs of the extreme left and indicating an unwillingness to launch another big push which would require large long-term borrowing from abroad. If the Chinese—contrary to my expectations—were to adopt either another round of radical attacks on the economic development problem or a big push with excessive rates of investment and emphasis on heavy industry, we would be forced, of course, to return to the drawing board for a new set of estimates of potential economic growth in China, as well as a new set of estimates of potential Sino-American trade.

The resulting estimates for economic growth in China over the fifteen years between 1965 and 1980 are indicated by the following quotation from the paper referred to above.

... Subject to the many assumptions that must be made to obtain these results, the model predicts that, if the Chinese were to increase the level of investment by 10 percent a year (a higher ratio would soon get them in trouble), allocate about one-third of that investment to the agricultural sector (which would be accompanied by the self-provided investment of the peasants), and achieve an increase of 5 percent a year in the productivity of labor *in all sectors*, the following beneficial results would be possible. Between 1965 and 1980, the rate of investment would increase from 20 to 24 percent, the rate of growth of the economy would steadily increase from 7 to 9 percent, the industrial share in total output would increase from 30 to 40 percent, the level of unemployment would initially rise and then begin to decline, and the average per capita consumption of the agricultural labor force would increase. The increase in the average per capita consumption of the agricultural labor force would be very slow initially and would never be very rapid, but the average in 1980 would be 40 percent higher than it was in 1965 ... [9]

Whereas my estimates indicate a rate of growth of 7 to 9 percent between 1965 and 1980, recent estimates published by the U.S. government show China's GNP increasing at an annual rate of 8.8 percent in 1968-71.[10]

Putting the first assumption concerning the relationship between domestic economic activity and China's foreign trade together with the second concerning the expected developments in China's domestic economic activity, and allowing for a continuation in the downward trend in China's foreign trade participation rate due to the many economic and political factors mentioned earlier in the paper, China's foreign trade in 1980 is estimated at 4.9 billion U.S. dollars each way, with an average annual rate of growth of 6.4 percent. In 1968-71, China's foreign trade was growing at an annual rate of 6.6 percent. (See Table 8-1.)

The third step in obtaining estimates of potential Sino-American trade is to determine what commodity composition and direction of foreign trade is likely to emerge in the near future.[11] Except for the abnormally low levels of raw and processed foodstuffs exports during the agricultural crises in 1959-61 and in the ensuing years of recovery, 1962-64, these exports, including animal and vegetable materials and fats, have consistently accounted for about one-fourth of total exports, with cotton textiles being China's largest single export commodity. Of the remainder, exports of minerals, metals, and chemicals are of some importance, but exports of machinery and equipment, due to China's present level of economic development, and manufactures—such as bicycles, fountain pens, radios etc.—are relatively trivial entries in the commodity export statistics, despite the publicity they receive in Chinese publications and in the popular press in the West.

Using 1965-67 as the base period and relying on the past structure of the export trade and on expected developments in the domestic economy, I estimate that between the base period and 1980 exports of machinery and equipment and exports of manufactured consumers goods (excluding textiles) will experience a fivefold increase; but even at the end of the period they will account for only 12 percent of China's total exports. Exports of textiles will triple, accounting for 30 percent of the total at the end of the 1970s, while exports of minerals and metals and exports of animal and vegetable materials will increase two and one-half times, each of these import categories remaining a stable share of total exports, i.e., 10 percent. Exports of foodstuffs will double and, therefore, increase more slowly than total exports, but will still account for as much as one-third of China's total imports in 1980.

On the import side, imports of machinery and equipment and minerals and metals increased rapidly during the 1950s as a result of the domestic investment program—the former category accounting for about 35 percent, the latter 30 percent of China's total imports in 1960. The impact of the agricultural crisis following the Great Leap Forward, and the resulting excess capacity in industry and low rates of investment, reduced the importance of machinery and equipment and minerals and metals imports during the early 1960s. Foodstuffs, never a significant import during the 1950s, were an important means of sustaining minimum consumption levels following the crisis and accounted for one-fourth of China's total imports in 1961-64. While these cereal imports have remained at a somewhat steady level ever since—reflecting, I believe, a wise choice of supplying the coastal urban population in North China with wheat in the face of unstable wheat production on the North China plain—they have steadily declined as a share of total imports as China's foreign trade revived at the end of the 1960s.

With the resumption of normal growth in the domestic economy following the Cultural Revolution, imports of machinery and equipment and minerals and metals have experienced very rapid growth and have regained their former position of dominance in China's trade. Due to the effects of the policy of import substitution during the past two decades, however, the share of machinery and equipment and that of minerals and metals have reversed their standings in China's import trade since the 1950s—the former accounting for 25 percent, the latter for 35 percent of China's total imports at the present time. Of the remainder of China's imports, chemicals—especially imports of fertilizers—have increased rapidly with the change in policy favoring the supply of current inputs to the agricultural sector following the agricultural crises. Thus, chemical imports now account for approximately 15 percent of China's total imports. All of these trends are expected to continue in the future so that at the end of the 1970s, imports of minerals and metals will account for 30 percent, machinery and equipment for 25 percent, chemicals for 15 percent, animal and vegetable materials for 10 percent, and foodstuffs for 5 percent of China's total imports.

Sino-American Trade Potential:
Statistical Estimates

It is relatively simple to show that the emerging direction of China's foreign trade would foster trade ties between China and the United States. Faced with an embargo made effective by the Battle Act, which cut off United States aid to any country supplying China with "strategic" goods, three-fourths of China's foreign trade in 1954 was with Communist countries, over one-half with the Soviet Union alone. China received no new loans from the Soviet Union after 1954, and the steady weakening of the embargo, due to the diminishing dependence of the non-Communist industrial countries on United States aid, led to a slight diversion of China's trade in favor of the industrialized countries of Western Europe, with those countries more than doubling their share of China's foreign trade between 1954 and 1958.

The Chinese initially believed that the Great Leap Forward was a success, providing them with sufficient export capacity to finance their imports from the Communist countries. Thus, in 1959, there was a significant switch back to trade with the Soviet Union at the expense of China's trade with Western Europe. The failure of the Great Leap and the ensuing agricultural crisis, however, reduced China's demands for producers goods obtainable in the Communist countries, and increased the demand for foodstuffs obtainable in the West. Therefore, in 1960, China's foreign trade reverted back to the West and away from the Communist countries. This economic cause of a change in the direction of China's foreign trade was strongly reinforced by the break in political relations with the Soviet Union. Therefore, by 1970, the Communist countries accounted for only 20 percent of China's total trade, while the developed countries of Western Europe and Asia accounted for one-half of the total. Of the remainder, the less-developed non-Communist countries account for 20 percent and Hong Kong for 10 percent of China's total trade. There is no indication of changes in the present direction of China's foreign trade. In addition, there are good reasons to believe China does not want to depend on a single dominant supplier of producers goods or rely on large-scale loans from abroad. Finally, political differences have not served as a major deterrent to trade with China. Thus, the existing and expected future direction of trade does not preclude a significant level of Sino-American trade. This conclusion is borne out by the initial Chinese reaction to the recent removal of US legal prohibitions on trade with China.

To estimate potential Sino-American trade, then, we are left with the problem of matching up the potential level and structure of Chinese export supplies and import demands.[12] The method used for this stage of the exercise is straightforward. On the United States import side, three estimates are made. The first merely states the Chinese will not react to the changes in legal restrictions and will sell nothing to the United States. This possibility is not only ruled out by common sense, it has already been proven wrong by the available empirical evidence. The second estimate assumes China will be able to achieve a share in the United States import market for the eight largest Chinese export commodities equal to the average shares China achieved for those same commodities in 1965-67 in the import markets of West Europe and Japan, resulting in an estimate of 200 million U.S. dollars for United States imports from China in 1980. A final estimate assumes China will be able to achieve a market share in total United States imports equal to the market share China achieved in 1965-67 in the total imports of western Europe and Japan, resulting in an estimate of 250 million U.S. dollars for total imports from China in 1980. Thus, in my earlier paper on potential Sino-American trade, I suggested $200 to $250 million as my estimate for potential United States imports from China in 1980. Some businessmen have argued my estimate is probably double the actual potential United States purchases from China, while an equal number have criticized me for being conservative, but I am willing to stick with this estimate until actual developments indicate that it is wrong.

On the United States export side, four estimates are made. As on the import side, the first estimate merely assumes the Chinese will not take advantage of the trade liberalization to purchase United States exports, an estimate already ruled out by developments since the change in the United States regulations on trade with China. The second estimate assumes the Chinese will pursue a policy of bilateral balance in trade with the United States, i.e., Chinese imports from the United States in 1980 will equal whatever we estimate their exports to the United States will be in 1980. While probably true for their foreign trade as a whole, except for trade with Japan, the Chinese have not maintained a balanced trade in bilateral exchanges with the non-Communist industrial countries. Japan is an exception because China's trade with that country was regulated by a bilateral barter agreement between the Chinese trading corporations and "friend-ly" Japanese firms to avoid the need to finance the trade through letters of credit drawn on banks in London. This arrangement, however, broke down after 1966, and China's imports exceeded exports in trade with Japan in 1967-71 by more than 450 million U.S. dollars. In any event, China's present trade negotiations with United States exporters certainly reveals a willingness of the Chinese to incur a bilateral import surplus in trade with the United States.

To obtain the other two estimates for potential United States exports to China in the near future, we estimated the probable trends in the structure and level of China's import trade and the share held by the United States in the world market for the commodities China will be importing. To make the analysis manageable, we limited our study to China's imports of minerals and metals and of machinery and equipment, which account for over 50 percent of China's total imports. Our third estimate is obtained by assuming, on the basis of the empirical evidence of the past, that the non-Communist industrialized countries will supply 60 percent of China's imports of minerals and metals and 50 percent of China's imports of machinery and equipment. The United States, if it is able to achieve its existing market shares in world trade in these commodities, would be able to achieve a level of exports to China in 1980 of $325 million. But exports in these two broad categories account for only 60 percent of the exports of the non-Communist industrialized countries to China, 50 percent of total United States exports. Finally, our fourth estimate for potential United States exports to China is obtained by doubling our third estimate so as to include other commodities not included in the analysis for minerals and metals and machinery and equipment, resulting in an estimate of $650 million. An estimate of potential United States exports to China in 1980 of between 325 and 650 million U.S. dollars is consistent with actual developments in Sino-American trade in the past few years.

Sino-American Trade Potential: Interpretation

The results of this mechanical exercise, a potential for exports from China to the United States of $200 to $250 million and exports to China from the United States of $325 to $650 million, while consistent with current developments, must be interpreted with care.

First, my statistical analysis of China's future export and import trade clearly indicated China's supply of exports and demand for imports could be accommodated by China's existing trade partners. Thus, the United States will have to compete in the China market with our many rivals in world trade. Two arguments will work in our favor, however. China is urgently seeking Western technology, and the United States has been designated explicitly by the Chinese as a major source of that technology. In this regard, much will depend on the future attitude of the United States government toward approving the supply of that technology to China. Furthermore, the United States is obviously being used by the Chinese for political purposes *vis-à-vis* the Russians, with Moscow Radio taking strong exception to the recent Chinese moves toward trade with the United States and making it clear that the Soviet Union is willing and able to supply China with her needs in the areas of advanced technology and physical capital.

Second, while my estimates of potential Sino-American trade indicate a relatively low level of trade (5 percent of China's total sales, 13 percent of China's total purchases, and an insignificant share of total United States trade), the potential China market for an individual United States producer could still be huge, especially if negotiations are held with a single representative of that market as a whole. This is especially true for United States producers of transport equipment, power plant equipment, construction machinery, machine tools, mining equipment, metallurgical plant equipment, oil field and refining equipment, petrochemicals, fertilizers, farm machinery, wheat, electronics equipment, telecommunications equipment, nonferrous metals, and iron and steel. Unfortunately, the Chinese state trading representatives of today can be as inscrutable as their Canton merchant guild ancestors, requiring the same skill, persistence, and patience of today's United States businessman that was exhibited by his ancestor who sold oil for the lamps of China. Unlike his ancestor, however, he is unlikely to benefit from recourse to gunboat diplomacy. Rather, the United States businessman trading with China undoubtedly will be called upon to play a major role in the creation of a new and more peaceful bridge between the two giants on either side of the Pacific.

Table 8-1
China's Total Trade, 1950-72 (nearest 5 million U.S. dollars)

Year	Total	Exports	Imports	Balance
1950	1210	620	590	30
1951	1900	780	1120	−340
1952	1890	875	1015	−140
1953	2295	1040	1255	−215
1954	2350	1060	1290	−230
1955	3035	1375	1660	−285
1956	3120	1635	1485	150
1957	3055	1615	1440	175
1958	3765	1940	1825	115
1959	4290	2230	2060	170
1960	3990	1960	2030	− 70
1961	3020	1530	1495	35
1962	2675	1525	1150	375
1963	2770	1570	1200	370
1964	3220	1750	1470	280
1965	3880	2035	1845	190
1966	4245	2210	2035	175
1967	3895	1945	1950	− 5
1968	3765	1945	1820	125
1969	3860	2030	1830	200
1970	4220	2045	2175	−130
1971	4660	2405	2255	150

Source: U.S. Central Intelligence Agency, *People's Republic of China: International Trade Handbook* (Washington: CIA publication A72-38, December 1972), p. 9.

Table 8-2
China's Direction of Trade, 1966-71 (nearest one million U.S. dollars)

	1966		1967		1968		1969		1970		1971	
	Exports	Imports	Exports	Imports	Exports	Imports	Exports	Imports	Exports	Imports	Exports	Imports
Total	2210	2035	1945	1950	1945	1820	2030	1830	2045	2175	2405	2255
Non-Communist	1625	1530	1460	1605	1445	1480	1540	1535	1570	1825	1825	1820
Japan	300	311	266	303	222	345	239	415	255	600	322	607
France	48	111	40	102	51	119	65	45	57	97	67	125
Italy	52	61	49	89	43	83	57	71	56	76	56	71
U.K.	82	96	68	135	71	70	79	132	69	143	69	92
W. Germany	82	135	65	231	76	196	78	202	70	200	89	160
Canada	20	195	25	105	25	160	27	129	22	154	28	213
Hong Kong	377	3	291	1	310	1	326	1	354	5	428	3
Communist	585	505	485	345	500	340	490	295	475	350	580	435
U.S.S.R.	145	175	55	50	35	60	30	25	20	25	75	80

Source: U.S. Central Intelligence Agency, *People's Republic of China: International Trade Handbook*, p. 11.

Table 8-3
China's Major Trading Partners, by Rank (total turnover, million U.S. dollars)

	1971	1970	1969	1968	1967	1966
Japan	1 (929)	1 (855)	1 (654)	1 (567)	1 (569)	1 (631)
Hong Kong	2 (431)	2 (359)	2 (327)	2 (34)	3 (292)	2 (380)
W. Germany	3 (249)	3 (270)	3 (280)	3 (272)	2 (296)	4 (217)
Canada	4 (241)	6 (176)	7 (156)	5 (185)	9 (130)	5 (215)
France	5 (192)	8 (154)	9 (110)	6 (170)	7 (142)	7 (159)
Malaysia-Singapore	6 (185)	5 (190)	4 (260)	4 (220)	6 (185)	8 (145)
United Kingdom	7 (161)	4 (212)	5 (211)	8 (141)	5 (203)	6 (178)
U.S.S.R.	8 (155)	22 (45)	19 (55)	10 (95)	10 (105)	3 (320)
Romania	9 (145)	10 (108)	14 (81)	15 (84)	14 (72)	19 (66)
Italy	10 (127)	9 (132)	8 (128)	9 (126)	8 (138)	10 (113)

Source: U.S. Central Intelligence Agency, *People's Republic of China: International Trade Handbook*, p. 14.

Table 8-4
China's Commodity Composition of Trade: Exports (nearest 5 million U.S. dollars)

	1966	1967	1968	1969	1970	1971
Total	2210	1945	1945	2030	2045	2405
Foodstuffs	615	510	535	615	645	790
Crude Materials	480	405	415	450	430	490
Chemicals	90	90	85	90	105	130
Textiles	305	250	270	310	340	325
Clothing	185	170	180	195	155	155

Source: U.S. Central Intelligence Agency, *People's Republic of China: International Trade Handbook*, p. 17.

Table 8-5
China's Commodity Composition of Trade: Imports (nearest 5 million U.S. dollars)

	1966	1967	1968	1969	1970	1971
Total	2035	1950	1820	1830	2175	2255
Foodstuffs	510	380	410	350	355	300
Crude Materials	340	320	300	310	360	355
Fertilizer	155	200	200	205	230	200
Iron and Steel	225	320	265	275	405	475
Nonferrous Metals	55	85	125	225	210	145
Machinery	455	380	275	240	395	495

Source: U.S. Central Intelligence Agency, *People's Republic of China: International Trade Handbook*, p. 19.

Notes

1. Simon Kuznets, "Quantitative Aspects of the Economic Growth of Nations," published in 10 parts in various issues of *Economic Development and Cultural Change* between 1956 and 1966.

2. Robert F. Dernberger, "Foreign Trade and Capital Movements of Communist China, 1949-1962," (Ph.D. dissertation, Harvard University, 1965), p. 108.

3. U.S. Central Intelligence Agency, *People's Republic of China: International Trade Handbook* (Washington: CIA, publication A72-38, December 1972), p. 1.

4. Robert F. Dernberger and Nicholas Lardy, "Future Sino-American Trade and Its Impact on China's Asian Trading Partners," paper presented at the Annual Meetings of the Association of Asian Studies, New York, March 1972.

5. "China Foreign Trade in 1971," vol. 10, *Current Scene*, October 1972, pp. 4, 6, 8.

6. There are seven state trading corporations handling China's foreign trade with the West: the China National Machinery Import and Export Corporation, the China National Chemicals Import and Export Corporation, the China National Metals and Minerals Import and Export Corporation, the China National Textile Import and Export Corporation, the China National Cereals, Oils and Foodstuffs Import and Export Corporation, the China National Light Industrial Products Import and Export Corporation, and the China National Native Products and Animal By-Products Import and Export Corporation. These corporations, operating in various major port cities in China, also have agents in Hong Kong and abroad.

7. Robert F. Dernberger, "Prospects for Trade Between China and the United States," in Alexander Eckstein, ed., *China Trade Prospects and US Policy* (New York: Praeger, 1971), pp. 183-319.

8. Robert F. Dernberger, "Conflicting Goals and Limited Possibilities: The Economic Dilemma of Modern China," in progress. The economic model of the Chinese economy referred to was first developed in an attempt to estimate the past, present, and future real costs of defense expenditures in China as part of a project sponsored by the U.S. Arms Control and Disarmament Agency.

9. Robert F. Dernberger, "Prospects for Trade Between China and the United States," op. cit., p. 221.

10. Robert F. Dernberger, "Radical Ideology and Economic Development in China: The Cultural Revolution and Its Impact on the Economy," *Asian Survey*, vol. 7, December 1972, p. 1060.

11. Statistics for the commodity composition of China's foreign trade in this and the following paragraph are based on estimates presented in the tables in Robert F. Dernberger, "Prospects for Trade Between China and the United States," op. cit.

12. For the derivation of these estimates, see Robert F. Dernberger, "Prospects for Trade Between China and the United States," op. cit.

Determinants of the Commodity Pattern of U.S. Trade—Policies for the 1970s

Robert E. Baldwin
University of Wisconsin—Madison

Traditional Trade Theory

Since the theory of comparative advantage was first expounded by David Ricardo more than 150 years ago, the main task of economists specializing on the real side of international trade has been to develop a theory explaining why a country exports a certain set of commodities and imports another. In other words, the question to be answered is what determines the particular commodity pattern of a country's international trade. In this chapter, I should like to discuss various suggested answers to this question, with special reference to United States trade, and also to explore some of the implications of these answers for United States trade policy.

The Ricardian theory of comparative costs states that a country will specialize in producing and exporting commodities in which its labor productivity is higher than the labor productivity in the same commodities in other countries. This means, for example, that even if labor productivity in a country is absolutely higher than in the rest of the world for all commodity production, it will still pay the country in real income terms to export the set of goods in which its productivity is the highest and import those goods at the lower end of its productivity scale. The main approach that has been followed in testing this theory has been to compare ratios of the exports of two countries to a third country for some set of goods with the ratios of labor productivities in the two countries for these goods. The rationale is that the higher a country's labor productivity for a certain good compared to that of other countries, the lower will be its unit costs and prices for that commodity compared to other countries. This in turn will tend to give the country a high share of the market in third countries for this commodity.

Tests of this proposition using United States and United Kingdom data yield strong support for the relationship that a country's market share of a particular commodity tends to be comparatively high when its labor productivity in this commodity is comparatively high. However, when the relationship between labor productivity ratios and relative export price ratios is tested directly, no significant relationship emerges. This finding casts doubt on the significance of the relationship between export shares and relative labor productivity. More fundamentally, labor productivity itself is not an exogenous variable, but influenced by the pattern of specialization itself. As Johnson has remarked, "... a correlation of relative market shares with relative labor productivities must very largely be a correlation of two measures of the consequences of comparative advantage with one another."[1] Furthermore, when we drop Ricardo's assumption that labor is the only productive factor and recognize the importance of human and physical capital, there is no longer any reason for focusing on relative labor productivity rather than on relative capital productivity. Actually, what should be considered within a Ricardian framework is a comparison between countries of total factor productivity.

The Ricardian theory of comparative costs, in addition to raising analytical and empirical problems, fails to offer any explanation of why factor productivities differ among countries. These differences are simply assumed. Since we are interested in understanding the causes of trade mainly because we can then take policy actions that help achieve our goals in the trade field, the Ricardian approach is deficient in that it does not go back far enough in trying to understand the nature of international trade.

Another approach to trade theory which does not have this drawback and has in fact been the most commonly accepted theory until recent years is the Heckscher-Ohlin factor-proportions theory of international trade. Heckscher laid out the essentials of the theory in 1919, and a student of his, Ohlin, refined and elaborated upon it in a book published in 1933. The factor-proportions theory can be stated very succinctly: a country tends to specialize in and exports commodities whose production requires relatively large amounts of the factors that are relatively abundant in the country. The logic of this theory is quite simple. First, we know that commodities differ with regard to the composition of the factors required for their production. Some commodities tend, for example, to require relatively large amounts of capital relative to labor. Machinery and automobile production are illustrations of capital-intensive activities. On the other hand, commodities such as textiles and shoes are produced labor-intensively. Of course, the actual capital/labor ratio employed in producing a commodity also depends upon the relative prices of capital and labor. But over a wide range of factor prices, the first set of goods tends to be produced more capital-intensively than the second set. In addition to focusing on the technological differences among commodities, the factor-proportions theory utilizes the relationship between factor proportions and factor prices. Factors that are in relatively abundant supply in a country tend to be relatively cheap in the country. For example, if the amount of capital per worker is high in one country compared to another, then in the absence of trade between the two countries, the cost of capital relative to labor will be lower in the first country than in the second. As is intuitively obvious, this will tend to give the first country a comparative cost advantage over the second country in producing capital-intensive goods. Conversely, the second country will tend to have a relative cost advantage in producing the second commodity.

The Heckscher-Ohlin theory represented a satisfying improvement over the Ricardian single-factor approach to the cause of international trade and quickly became generally accepted after Ohlin's book was published in the early 1930s. Simply on the basis of casual empiricism, it also seemed to be correct. Everyone knew, for example, that the United States was the most capital-abundant country in the world. Moreover, we exported such items as machinery and automobiles, which are both produced in a comparatively capital-intensive fashion, and imported such commodities as textiles and shoes, whose production uses relatively high ratios of labor to capital. Thus, it seemed that the United States exported comparatively capital-intensive goods and imported relatively labor-intensive commodities in accord with the Heckscher-Ohlin factor-proportions theory.

Leontief's Paradoxical Results

This theory was not tested in any rigorous fashion until Wassily Leontief undertook such an effort in the early 1950s. By utilizing the U.S. 1947 input-output table, Leontief was able to determine the amount of capital and labor used directly and indirectly in producing a representative bundle of United States exports. Similarly, he was able to find out how much capital and labor would be needed to produce a representative bundle of imports in the United States instead of purchasing them from abroad. Leontief fully expected to find that a higher ratio of capital to labor was required for United States exports than for import-replacing production and undertook the exercise to demonstrate what could be done with input-output tables, a tool whose use he had pioneered. To his surprise, he obtained the opposite result. United States import-competing production was capital-intensive compared to her export production. The initial reaction of most trade economists was that his results must represent a special case. For example, he used 1947 trade data which was quite atypical of the United States long-run trade pattern, since it was so near the end of World War II. He also did not break the trade data down as finely as was possible, and some thought this may have caused an aggregation bias. Consequently, he retested the Heckscher-Ohlin hypothesis using 1951 trade data, although still employing the 1947 input-output coefficients, and divided traded goods into 192 groups. He still found that the United States paradoxically exported labor-intensive commodities, even though there is no doubt we are the most capital abundant nation in the world. Subsequently, I tested the hypothesis using the U.S. 1958 input-output table and 1962 trade data. This test confirmed Leontief's earlier results. In further tests, which are still preliminary, I used the 1963 input-output table and the 1969 trade pattern and still found our exports are produced labor-intensively compared to what factor proportions would be required to produce a representative bundle of imports in the United States rather than importing these goods.

The Leontief paradox represents a major challenge to trade economists, for it runs counter to a theory that had long been accepted by them with little question. The problem before us has been to come up with new theories which, when empirically tested, are consistent with the actual pattern of United States trade. A useful way to proceed to this task is first to examine the assumptions necessary for the Heckscher-Ohlin theory to be logically valid, and then proceed to try to ascertain whether the failure of any of these assumptions to hold could produce the Leontief result.

Let me start by considering certain assumptions of the Heckscher-Ohlin theory that do not seem to be at the source of the Leontief paradox. One is that tastes must be identical among all trading countries and income demand-elasticities be unity. If this assumption does not hold, it could be the case that the United States has such a strong preference towards consuming capital-intensive goods compared to other countries that we not only produce relatively more of these goods than our trading partners, but even import them. Now, of course, we know that tastes are not identical among countries. Nonetheless, there is no evidence to indicate that taste differences are sufficiently large to be the cause of the Leontief paradox. Indeed, in my tests of the theory, I found that because the United States per capita income is higher than in the rest of the world, U.S. imports tend to shift toward labor-intensive rather than capital-intensive commodities.[2] A second, somewhat more technical possible explanation for the failure of the Heckscher-Ohlin theory to hold for U.S. trade is that commodities may be produced capital-intensively at one set of factor prices and labor-intensively at another. This means that the nature of technology runs counter to what the Heckscher-Ohlin theory implicitly assumes, namely, that a commodity is capital-intensive relative to other commodities at all possible relative factor prices. Some studies in the early 1960s suggested that within relevant factor prices this assumption was in fact widely violated. It would then be possible for both the United States and the rest of the world to export labor-intensive goods, and thus the Heckscher-Ohlin theory would not be meaningful. Subsequent studies have indicated that the violations of the Heckscher-Ohlin technology are much fewer than initially thought, and it now seems doubtful that widespread factor-intensity reversals are the cause of the Leontief paradox.

The Role of Educated Labor in U.S. Trade

Much more promising as explanations of the observed United States trade pattern than demand bias or factor-intensity reversals are differences in labor skills and differences in technology among countries. The simple version of the Heckscher-

Ohlin model assumes that there is only one type of labor and that its quality is uniform among countries. Yet we know, in fact, that skills vary widely within and among countries. Since to a large extent skills are acquired through formal or on-the-job training, which represents an investment in individuals, a useful way to view differences in skills is to consider them differences in supplies of human capital. The United States may be capital-abundant but, instead of using all of this capital for plant and equipment, it embodies part of the capital in individuals in the form of human skills. The United States may be relatively well-endowed with human skills, and therefore within the Heckscher-Ohlin framework it would be expected that we would export goods requiring relatively large amounts of skilled labor. As country comparisons of average years of schooling and other crude measures indicate, we are in fact well-endowed with skilled labor. Furthermore, when the United States labor force is divided into anywhere from five to eleven skill groups, and when the labor requirements for each of these skill groups are determined for sixty-four traded commodity classes, it turns out that our exports do require relatively larger amounts of skilled labor than our imports. Similarly, our imports compared to our exports embody relatively large amounts of unskilled labor. When labor used in production of the various commodities is classified by years of education, the human capital explanation is again supported. Our list of net export items compared to our import list is weighted toward products using large amounts of highly educated labor. Average years of education of export workers as well as the actual average costs of educating these workers also are higher than for workers employed in import-competing industries. Still another bit of evidence in support of this relationship is that average wages are higher in export industries than those in which there is a net import surplus.

The implication of this relationship for future economic policy of the United States is obvious. If we are to maintain a vigorous export position in world trade and in particular avoid very painful adjustments within our economy, it is important that we continue to remain near the top among countries in terms of formal and informal educational systems. There is no mystery as to why we enjoy a high standard of living compared to most of the other residents of the world. It is not because we are endowed with especially favorable supplies of natural resources or because we are especially intelligent or hard-working. Basically, it is because we possess much higher educational and skill levels than most other countries.[3] This has a twofold economic effect. Because of the relatively abundant supplies of skilled labor of all sorts, the relative price of this type of labor is comparatively low, and we therefore have a comparative advantage in the production of goods requiring this type of labor. Secondly—and this is a point that I want to deal with presently in some detail—our high level of education enables us to discover new and better ways of producing goods and thereby continually raise our living standards.

In view of the importance of our educational system in maintaining a vigorous export position and continually rising living standards in general, it is somewhat alarming to observe the downgrading that higher education is receiving as a policy objective among many politically significant groups. Because it has a long payoff period and consequently can be reduced with little immediate damage, higher education is being cut back in favor of such goals as a better distribution of income and improvements in our environmental conditions. While these are important and worthy goals, I would suggest that better educational facilities can also help to implement these goals. Providing better education for low-income and minority groups benefits these groups and the country as a whole. Similarly, better technology as a result of education and research can help significantly in our efforts to improve our environment.

The importance of greater efforts to improve our training and educational facilities is brought out by considering the problem of reemploying workers who lose their jobs from import competition. A study by the Labor Department indicates that the average period of unemployment of these workers is about nine months. Over this period, these workers receive only unemployment compensation, and the nation as a whole loses the output they formerly contributed. One of the major reasons why these workers cannot readily find new jobs is that many do not possess the requisite skills to compete successfully in the modern industrial society. We must provide the educational facilities to improve upon these existing conditions and thereby help the workers themselves and our economy in general.

The Role of Technology in U.S. Trade

As I noted, another by-product of greater educational efforts, particularly at the higher levels, is technological progress. The Heckscher-Ohlin trade theory does not stress this factor as an independent determinant of trade patterns because the theory assumes that technological knowledge is everywhere the same. Just as the assumption of homogeneous labor among countries is not appropriate, so too is it incorrect to assume that the state of technological knowledge is the same among countries. Empirical work strongly supports the view that the comparative advantage of the United States in certain lines of production rests on our ability to come up with product and production improvements in these lines on a continuing basis. A rough measure of these continuing efforts to improve technology is the extent of research and development (R and D) activities among industries. Several investigators have found that the United States industries which tend to have a high share of world export markets are those in which R and D efforts, measured either by actual expenditures or by the relative importance of scientists and engineers in an industry, are comparatively large. In my studies, the R and D variable invariably showed up as highly significant in multi-regression analysis of the United States trade structure.[4]

Studies of individual industries have further supported the view that this is a very important variable in explaining United States trade. A group at the Harvard Business School led by Raymond Vernon has found evidence of a product cycle in certain industries. The cycle proceeds along the following lines: United States industry first discovers a new product and then gradually perfects it by focusing primarily on the United States market. The large size of this market and its proximity is ideal for this product development. At this stage, foreign demand is satisfied by exporting the product from the United States. However, as the product becomes perfected and as foreign markets grow, it now becomes profitable to satisfy the foreign market by establishing production facilities in high income countries abroad. More and more this takes the form of an affiliate within the multinational corporation framework rather than of leasing patents to foreign companies. In this second stage, besides serving markets within the countries where production facilities are set up, the overseas affiliates supply a growing share of other foreign markets. Finally, in stage three when the technology is completely standardized, production units are established in the low-income, low-wage countries and exports are sent from these countries back to the United States. The U.S. firm drops most of its production and concentrates on products in the first stage of the cycle.

One of the hard facts that we in this country must face is that a combination of growing labor skills abroad and certain technological developments themselves have accelerated the pace at which foreign countries are catching up with United States technology. Now, teams can be quickly sent to foreign affiliates to iron out production and marketing problems. We, in effect, can easily combine United States technology and high level United States managerial and technical labor with cheap, conscientious foreign labor. For productive lines such as electronics, where the semi-skilled labor requirements are extensive, United States direct investment in such countries as Mexico, Taiwan, and Hong Kong represents the most profitable way to serve the home market.

The recent reductions in governmental and private grants for pure and applied research directly reduce our ability to maintain a strong export position and to adjust to the effects of rapidly expanding technological knowledge abroad. Fortunately, there seems to be a growing awareness of the importance of technological progress in maintaining growing living standards in the United States, but so far this is insufficient to change the anti-technology trend in attitudes in this country. The AFL-CIO, for example, supports a bill before Congress that would empower the President to prevent the exportation of technological knowledge if this embargo would lead to greater employment within the United States. Since the transmission of technology abroad is a major source of profits for United States firms—indeed it is useful to regard this transmission as a major United States export activity—such a prohibition is very likely to reduce the rate of new discoveries. One should not conclude, however, that United States labor does not have a valid concern. They do, in the sense

that severe hardships are being imposed on certain workers because of the flow
of technical knowledge abroad. But the inward-looking policy of the AFL-CIO is
not the best way to handle this problem, in my view. First, as I have already
noted, we need greater training and planning efforts to minimize the hardships
imposed on these workers from rapid increases in imports from abroad.
Secondly, we should be encouraging greater research activities at all levels rather
than discouraging them. This will enable new products to replace the old and
thereby reduce the shock on the United States economy when products
originally discovered here are produced abroad and imported into this country.

The Role of Foreign Natural
Resources in U.S. Trade

Another important explanation of Leontief's paradoxical results relates to our
increasing reliance on foreign natural resources. In looking for the reason why
United States imports are more capital-intensive than our exports, one soon
discovers that we have a net import surplus in several important mineral
categories, and that these items are produced capital-intensively. The production
of crude oil is highly capital-intensive, for example. Another fact striking one
with regard to United States imports of natural resource products is that United
States firms abroad are involved in this transfer. In other words, United States
capital and technology have flowed abroad to develop foreign natural resources
in order to supply the home market. The Heckscher-Ohlin theory assumes the
absence of any factor movements between countries. But the violation of this
assumption can mean that some countries are exporting natural resource
products to the United States not because they possess both rich natural
resources and a plentiful supply of capital, but because they have rich natural
resources and are supplied with United States capital to develop them. In a
sense, one should exclude this type of trade when testing the Heckscher-Ohlin
trade theory.

One of the tests Leontief described in his second article[5] was to exclude
nineteen industries which he rather arbitrarily termed "natural resource"
industries. This was the only case in which he was able to reverse the paradox
and obtain the expected result. In my tests using the 1958 input-output table,
the exclusion of these same industries reduced the difference between the
capital-intensity of United States imports and exports, but imports still remained
somewhat more capital-intensive. However, in my latest tests using the 1963
table, the expected result is obtained when these industries are omitted,
although the difference in favor of export industries is not very large. The role of
imports of natural resource products in accounting for the overall capital-intensity of United States imports compared to exports is further brought out by
breaking down United States trade figures on a geographic basis. One finds that

our trade with both Western Europe and Japan conforms to the expected Heckscher-Ohlin results, namely, that exports are more capital-intensive than imports. It is our trade with Canada and the Less Developed Countries, where imports of mineral products are so important, that produces the opposite result and causes the paradoxical outcome on total trade.

Two comments are in order concerning our trade in natural resource products, one relating to policy matters and the other to the need for further research. As for the policy implications of this trade, the growing scarcity of minerals within this country implies that our future imports will be even more heavily weighted by these products, so that our imports may become even more capital-intensive compared to our exports. This growing dependence on imports of raw materials to keep our industrial system functioning smoothly also reenforces the importance of maintaining our human capital and technological advantage in international trade. We must export in order to obtain key imports, and unless we can maintain a high foreign demand for our exports, the cost of importing will be high enough to cause painful readjustments within the United States economy.

The point concerning further research relates to the need to broaden our theory of international trade to include international movements of commodities, capital, labor, and technology. The standard framework which assumes that capital and labor do not move across borders and that technology is everywhere the same is woefully inadequate in coping with the problems of the present world economy. The concepts of imperfect markets and differentiated products must also replace the typical assumption of perfect competition and standardized products. The growth in the importance of the multinational corporation illustrates the need for these changes. The multinational corporation now considers the alternative of servicing a foreign market by exporting or by sending technology, top managers, technicians, and capital abroad to establish foreign production facilities. Moreover, as the product-cycle theory points out, there seems to be regular pattern in many cases with respect to shipping the product or the knowledge and productive factors needed to produce it abroad. We must discover just what factors determine whether productive factors or commodities are traded, and—most important—we must substantiate our answer by careful empirical analysis.

Commercial Policy and U.S. Trade

A final factor that may account for a significant part of the Leontief result is trade-distorting commercial policy. For example, if we impose high import duties on labor-intensive products, the share of these items in our total import list will be smaller than under free trade conditions. The production of a representative bundle of imports will, in turn, involve a higher capital-labor ratio than under free trade conditions. If, at the same time, foreign countries are protecting their capital-intensive products, United States exports of capital-intensive goods will be relatively smaller than otherwise. Both of these protectionist policies tend to increase the capital-intensity of the United States imports relative to exports. My analysis of the United States tariff structure confirms that we do indeed protect labor-intensive industries more than capital-intensive ones.[6] Yet this protection does not appear to be so strong that it represents a major explanation of the Leontief paradox.

It is in our interest, however, to undertake reciprocal negotiations with other countries aimed at reducing trade barriers. This will enable us to concentrate on what we produce relatively best and thereby raise our living standards. In our trade negotiations we must concentrate on reducing barriers to trade *other than tariffs*. Average duty levels on dutiable industrial products are only about 10 percent in the major trading nations. However, there are still many so-called nontariff barriers to trade. Examples of these are import quotas, export subsidies, government purchasing policies that discriminate against foreigners, various types of domestic aids to particular industries, and administrative practices and regulations that unnecessarily penalize foreign sellers. When a country is facing stiff import and export competition, as the United States now is, it is tempting to handle the problem by imposing higher tariffs and quotas to keep foreign goods out of the country. There is considerable support in this country for this protectionist response. The AFL-CIO not only wants to prevent the outflow of new technological knowledge, but to impose import quotas on most manufactures that would keep the ratio of imports to domestic production at their 1965-69 levels. What happens over an extended period with these policies is that our productive resources become frozen in product lines where we are economically inefficient and where unemployment is often a chronic problem even without import competition. This, in turn, impairs our ability to shift resources into those export lines in which we have a potential comparative advantage and reduces our ability to compete internationally. As I have previously noted, in the future we must import more and more raw materials in order to keep our industrial society running smoothly. But if we cannot export, we will not be able to import, and the economy will decline in efficiency even further. In other words, there is a high long-run cost to an inward-looking protectionist policy.

The alternative is to face our trade problem squarely and take actions that mitigate the adjustment costs. One action that would be helpful would be a much expanded adjustment assistance program for workers whose jobs are threatened by import-competition. The new trade bill goes part-way in meeting this need but much more should be done in terms of planning the gradual elimination of excess capacity and of retraining displaced workers. Another needed change is the establishment of an international monetary system which provides much greater exchange-rate flexibility than existed under the old system. Personally, I think that the United States will have to depreciate the dollar gradually over time to meet our trade problems. If we do not reduce the foreign price of the dollar, we are likely to see recurrences of the currency crises that have plagued us within the last few years. Import-competing industries and export industries must come to realize currency depreciations are one of the best ways to adjust to their problems rather than being actions that in some sense are indications of failure on the part of government economic policies.

Summary

In summary then, an analysis of why the United States exports certain goods and imports others indicates that our competitive advantage is based on our human skills and our ability to produce rapid technological improvements with these skills. I think we must accept the conclusion that in the future other countries will continue to narrow our competitive advantage with respect to these factors. This is part of the process by which per capita income levels will be made more equal in the world, and we should welcome this prospect. Of course, this catching-up process will require significant adjustments in the structure of United States industry. But if we continue to push vigorously for educational programs that help us continue as the technological leader in the world, even though our leadership edge will not be as great as before, if we greatly strengthen our adjustment assistance programs, and if we adopt sensible exchange rate policies, I see no reason why the United States cannot adapt to the new international realities in a comparatively smooth and painless fashion.

Notes

1. H.G. Johnson, *Comparative Cost and Commercial Policy Theory for a Developing World*, Wiksell Lecture 1968 (Stockholm: Almqvist and Wiksell, 1968), p. 28.

2. Robert E. Baldwin, "Determinants of the Commodity Structure of US Trade," *American Economic Review*, vol. 61, March 1971, p. 139.

3. The natural resource factor was initially important, however, in generating the economic surplus that was used to provide the high level of education.

4. Baldwin, op. cit.

5. Wassily Leontief, "Factor Proportions and the Structure of American Trade," *Review of Economics and Statistics*, vol. 38, November 1956, pp. 386-407.

6. Baldwin, op. cit., p. 39.

About the Editors

Kenneth Jameson received the B.A. in history from Stanford University. After a two-year stay in Peru he enrolled in the University of Wisconsin-Madison, where he received the M.S. and the Ph.D. in Economics. Dr. Jameson has published articles in the *Quarterly Journal of Economics*, the *Review of Politics*, and the *Review of Social Economy*; he is a cowinner of the 1973 Kazanjian Foundation Award for Economics Education. Dr. Jameson is assistant professor of economics at the University of Notre Dame.

Roger Skurski received the B.A. from Cornell University and the M.A. and the Ph.D. from the University of Wisconsin. He has published articles in a number of journals, including *Slavic Review, Soviet Studies, Quarterly Review of Economics and Business*, and *The National Tax Journal.* Dr. Skurski is assistant professor of economics and Director of Graduate Studies in Economics at the University of Notre Dame.